Ghosts, Outlaws, Polygamists and DNA

DEDICATION

Butch, Sundance, Etta, Tom, Matt, Joshua, Bub
The Ghosts of the Wild Bunch
and their families

"The Utah Cousins"

Also dedicated to John Scarffe
Visionary Editor from Nederland, Colorado.

And to all the great people in my life who have loved me and
supported me on this grand adventure. I could not have made it
without all of you.

CONTENTS

ACKNOWLEDGMENTS

Thank you Grandpa Sundance. I cannot express enough thanks to my second great grandfather, William Henry Long. His companionship, his insights, his guidance and support were immeasurable. It's been one Wild Ride with the Ghost of Sundance.

A very special and sincere appreciation is well-deserved and earned the hard way goes to John Scarffe, of Nederland, Colorado. His untiring hours and hours of editing made all of this into an intelligent and much more interesting book. John's encouragement and belief in me helped me more than I can express. Grandpa Sundance has a special thanks for John who helped me when no one else would. John held this vision with me until it became real.

My deepest appreciation goes to my brothers who were riding the Outlaw Trail right alongside me or making my web pages and videos with whatever I could stay focused enough to get home from Robbers Roost with. Better men are not found on this planet.

My completion of this project could not have been accomplished without the support of my husbands, my friends, my family and my Utah Cousins. There is a great legacy that is beginning to die off with each of our brothers and sisters who lived through an era of history where each person's contribution was highly significant.

Here in the West we had to take care of each other or we were doomed. We survived and learned to thrive. Our courage paid off, our fortitude got us through. Welcome to Utah, the only place where Ghosts, Outlaws, Polygamists and DNA could all come together and make a grand adventure that lives on and on each descendent.

The Utah Cousins know who they are, most of them, and the rest are invited to find out using my Outlaw Trail Adventures Ancestry Database on Ancestry.com. I was given these gifts by many wonderful cousins and friends and this is my way of giving back and sharing the adventures.

Enough talking...let's get on the trail.

CHAPTER 1

Dancing With the Ghost of Sundance

The Ghost of William Henry Long

"I've got one!" Joshua jumped up and down. "Oh, man, I've got one!"

He just wanted to talk to a ghost and two hours after a sincere prayer, he indeed connected with a ghost. "He's about my height (5' 9") or so, and adult in 1900, three-quarter length coat with a top hat and pointed shoes…a ghostly image from a high speed video showing a flash of his coat and pointed shoes…along with orbs of light rolling off.

The Ghost of William Henry Long had just introduced himself in a four-story abandoned dome rock house.

A mud bog aptly named "The Muddy Dubb". It was an area just below Rico, on the Delores River in Southwestern Colorado.

On this night, the 9th of May in the year 1891, bouncing baby Ernest Morrell made his way into this world. He was born in the buckboard of his parents, Luzernia and Silas Morrell's wagon on the Muddy Dubb.

"There are outlaws out there!" Bill hollered as he stumbled into camp. Blood was flowing out of his left leg from a gun-shot wound, Bill was bleeding out and dying. Luzernia jumped from the wagon where her 6 children and slowly dying husband were watching, took the black scarf from around Bill's neck and put a tourniquet on his leg…saving his life. This is the ghost Joshua met in the darkest of nights at creaking, abandoned house in Herriman, Utah.

In the 5 volume History of Rico, Colorado, it lists an attempted bank robbery on the night baby Ernest was born. The would be bank robbers capped the chimney which sent smoke through the bank. The attempt was foiled. There is no way from her to tell if there is a connection for sure, this is a worthy note until further light and knowledge comes by.

Connecting with the Past

Remote Viewer Bambie Reed explains the details of the first meeting with the ghost of William Henry Long.

"Let's help him heal," Joshua said about the ghost he could talk to that night. With my intuitive heart/mind connection I began a conversation with my ghost. He said, "I have lived a very harsh life."

The ghost's life began to unfold before my inner sight. He shared the darkness in his soul and showed me the essence of his life in the hope that I would help him heal and move into the light. It was darker than anything I've encountered in my life and I was moved with compassion to hold this healing space with him, for all he wanted now was to heal himself and his family and move into the light.

As his desire to move into the light was expressed, the beings of light came and as he moved on through Joshua, this man who had died in earlier part of 1900's began to synch with Joshua loving heart and mine. As the ghost moved on through, his heart got happier and happier and he went with the beings of light and all was well.

Joshua got to meet his ghost and I embarked upon an adventure which has been 10 years in the living. What began that night became Outlaw Trail Adventures and has taken me down a thousand foot sand cliff and into the remote reaches of Robbers Roost.

My Outlaw Trail Adventure with Grandpa Sundance has taken me to Bill Long's second funeral and this was his third burial all due to DNA searches and historically significant research and a little family feuding born of differing agendas. Ok, we're human.

The Proof Is In The Cow Pies...

DNA, where the cutting edge of science meets the paranormal arena of Ghosts, everybody had it the key is interpreting the data and applying to a real ghost hunt. Mix this with hard core research and voila…proof.

What began as so elusive is now on solid ground. Standing on the firm foundation of the science of DNA research coupled with genealogical research married to historical research, 10 years of research. It has been a most remarkable time of grand adventures.

It's time to put it all together and tell the world the most incredible stories of the real lives and families of Butch Cassidy, Sundance, Eta, Tom, Bill, Joshua, Bub. These are the members of the Wild Bunch who are all related. Yes, you heard me, related.

Bub is a cousin of a cousin of mine, Utah Cousin. We'll dive deep into what it means to be a Utah Cousin. Outside Utah, we are a rare breed. Insider stories and tales of adventure backed up by a 60,000 name genealogy data base all related to Sundance and Butch, Etta and the rest is being unleashed.

William Henry Long is my second great grandfather; he's also The Sundance Kid. I met his ghost one deep dark night in Herriman, Utah, at a haunted old rock round house that is now gone.

I promised him I would help he heal and move into the light. In the beginning there were possibilities. Everyone in the family had their beliefs about his true identity. In fact, I originally was helping my Uncle Jerry prove he was Harry Longabaugh.

The latest in scientific DNA testing found YDNA and the results of the comparison between Harry Longabaugh and William

Henry Long said NOT MATCH. Bill Long's YDNA and Harry Longabaugh's YDNA DO NOT MATCH!

At that point, I put on my boots and my spurs and started riding Outlaw Trail Adventures in pursuit of helping The Ghost of Sundance heal and move into the light. That's right. And this is how I came to ride with a bunch of Wild West Outlaw Loving Cowboys and Cowgirls. First it came down to serious research:

Outlaw Trail Adventures

Aliases (For The Sundance Kid) According to Wikipedia
- The Sundance Kid
- Frank Smith
- H.A. Brown
- Harry A. Place
- Harry **Long**

Get on your horses and ride with me on Outlaw Trail Adventures, if you dare. I'm about to give up the secrets which I have been led to by people, both alive and those who are dead, yes ghosts if you must say it to understand what I'm talking about.

Grimace if you must, hide if you have to; get excited if you have the courage. This is a grand adventure from which we will emerge people who have traveled hand in hand, heart to heart, shoulder to shoulder with those whose lives gave us our hopes, our dreams, our experiences.

Remote Viewer Bambie Reed Explains Dancing with the Ghost of Sundance

There are heroes and there are devils and most of us are somewhere in-between working out our lives. There are thrillers and there are killers and most of us are somewhere in-between work out our lives.

There are healers and there are stealers and most of us are somewhere in-between working out our lives. Most of us have stolen something for some important reason along the way.

Most of us have had to cross the line into shadow at some

point to accomplish something that could be reached no other way. In real life, the lines between right and wrong, good and evil, honor and dishonor are a matter of dealing with the givens in each moment.

"Dancing with the Ghost of Sundance" is about having respect for human experience. It's tough to be human some days and in some times. It's exquisite to be human other days. Most days are in-between. Mine is not to judge that which I have no ability to truly understand for I was not there for most of it. Would I have done anything differently?

We all watched Butch Cassidy and the Sundance Kid and most of us loved the beautiful Etta. As I talk to young people now, they often don't yet remember the female outlaw so beautiful and intriguing, mysterious to this day.

Yet she still draws us to her, wondering, asking, seeking to know her for those of us who know of her love her mystery and beauty, her courage and amazing representation of a history and a time that calls to us from the dark shadows of our souls...who is she?

If I start singing, "Raindrops keep falling on my head..." everyone remembers her from the movie riding on the bicycle wearing her white dress and we all feel warm and smile in remembrance.

So pull your warm blanket up around you while we sit at the camp fire and help me spin this yarn and fashion it after what really happened as close as we have the ability to recall from 115 years ago.

Etta's part of the story about Dancing with Sundance all started when the first train came into "The Cove", Sevier County, Utah. It's mighty engine roared across the brand spanken' new Red Covered Train Bridge across the Sevier River near Joseph, Utah. The Red Covered Train Bridge stood all these decades until about a 10 years ago when the Sevier River reached up and claimed it in a raging flood.

To this day you can see the moorings and the raised train beds in the 3 pointed turn that for about 6 years the train manipulated through to turn around and return north out of Sevier County. After that, Marysvale became the train central location in the area, bypassing the Cove.

6

In 1896, back when The Cove was in its heyday, there was a saloon, a livery stable, a hotel and a blacksmith shop. The saloon, livery stable, hotel and blacksmith shop have long ago disappeared through disintegration.

But there was one moment in time, one very magical moment when there was a Red Covered Train Bridge in the Sevier Valley of Utah and in 1896 the first train came down the tracks from Elsinore and Richfield up Marysvale Canyon not very far, reversed its engines and arched around across that red bridge into the train station in a Ghost Town named Cove, Utah.

It was only a viable town for 6 years or so, but in its heyday, it was quite the town. Feeding the Kimberly Mine, The Silver King Mine, and the other mines in the area, the train to Cove had a significant impact on everyone in the area at that time.

The train wasn't the only attraction the mouth of Marysvale Canyon in 1896. They say that everyone came to the dances held at the mouth of Marysvale Canyon where the dance floor among the trees on the bank of the Sevier River. By 1915 it was called The Shady Dell, but before that there were dances and everyone came, including Butch Cassidy.

How do we know this? My good friend and neighbor, Della Lee, who was raised in Circleville, Utah, and who dies only last year or so almost a centurion she had a tale to tell. Her father, whose last name was Nay, would ride on the buckboard of their family wagon with Butch Cassidy, that's right, THE BUTCH CASSIDY, when they would all get in the wagon and go to the dances at the Shady Dell or its predecessor.

The discovery about this amazing train station that existed for only a few years at the turn of the century is so fascinating, it's intrigue was only out classed by the people who met right there in Cove, Utah in 1896. Etta just happened to be living in the area when the first train came to Cove.

It was a very big deal to the Sevier County folks. It represented income and survival in oh so many ways. It also had a most remarkable man on board.

On the first train to Cove, Frank E. Smith rode into town where he met the love of his life, Julia ETTA Ames, and that meeting changed everything. Julia ETTA Ames was working at the boarding house in Cove when this handsome man rode in on the

7

first train to Cove.

He was tall, handsome and irresistible. Her breath stopped when she saw him. And he knew her good friend, Butch Cassidy, whom she had danced with in Milford, Utah. Her father had all but disowned her for dancing the night away with Butch back in Beaver Bottoms and Milford, Utah.

For two years a young and very beautiful Etta was kicking against the pricks and doing all she could to grow up and have more in life for herself and her future children. Her independence and choice of men to dance with angered her father, George Monteville Ames.

George was a freighter running freight from Payson, Utah to southern Utah. He greatly objected to his young and beautiful daughter hanging out with people he didn't approve of. He was adamant about "their type" not being good for her and he probably even moved her to Joseph, Utah, to live with her older sister, Rosina Ames Farnsworth to get her away from her suitors.

Wait, though. Who is this fascinating woman named Julietta Ames, or Julie **Etta** Smith as is engraved on her headstone in Price, Utah. We have substantial proof that Frank Smith who married Etta, Julietta Ames, Julia Etta Ames, is one of the people who took on the name The Sundance Kid.

The first powerful evidence is that he's married to an Etta. The Etta that Butch first fell love with and danced with in Milford, Utah. Now this Etta, the first Etta, was related through marriage. We'll show that relationship soon enough.

The second powerful evidence is that his name is Frank Smith, one of the main aliases for The Sundance Kid. Now, we know from his Y DNA tests that his DNA thinks he's from the Netherlands and likely a Smith.

We do have a strong lead as to who his DNA thinks he is and will be unfolding the discovery process to you as we progress with this great ghost story.

In the beginning of the DNA research for Frank Smith, his YDNA suggested he was a Terry. However, the Terry surname is a more distant connection both from the Netherlands. AND NO HE'S NOT A LONGABAUGH EITHER! SCIENCE PREVAILS!

What makes this a great ghost story? It's a real story based on meeting a real ghost. It's true confession time. I'm a psychic medium who does hypnosis and remote viewing. My main life focus is harmonic convergence with our highest creative intelligence. I believe we all came here with a highest calling in life and we have been given a set of givens in our lives.

The challenge for all of us is to take the givens we have been given and evolve this into our highest calling. At which point we experience our Optimal Life Experience and are living our greatest possibilities. To reach this amazing experience, I call it OLE', is really remarkable and feels so exquisite.

Musicians call it the zone, sports people call it the zone, computer geeks call it programming, poets know the experience, everyone I've met so far, have their experience of peak energies flowing where they are energized and focused beyond anything they've ever experienced before and EVERYONE WANTS TO BE IN THAT STATE ALWAYS IN ALL WAYS...It's the Ultimate Feel Great State.

Now, the beauty of this process is that once you awaken on the PATH (Portal Access to Hyperspace) you begin to experience OLE' every time you are connected to the Creative Intelligence which created us and lets us play here.

It is in the fulfillment of this process that our souls are fed, our minds enlivened beyond anything we've imagined before and our hearts are brought into harmony with our sacred space, heart space which awakens our heart intelligence.

To make it simple, Pure FUN! Raw and wriggling life, soul expanding, mind enhancing, heart space strengthening...fun, just pure fun of the best kind, that's what it is. It's only gets dicey when we are holding onto things that are of a lesser frequency than we can be experiencing if we so choose. It was this spiritual path that brought me to The Outlaw Trail. I know, amazing.

It's a Wild Ride! Just the perfect platform to bring in the adventure of a lifetime: Riding the Outlaw Trail with The Wild Bunch, Butch, Sundance, Etta, Tom, Bub, Joshua, Tom McCarty, Bill McCarty, and others.

These are just the ones who have come to me in ceremony and asked me to help them heal and return to the light. It started with Sundance, my second great grandfather and moved on through. Each of their stories is phenomenal and touching as I brought their stories forward, did their genealogy and began to see how interconnected we all are.

More importantly, how much we are interdependent on each other whether we want to acknowledge it or not, make it useful or leave valuable resources and life gifts from "the spirit of creation" on the table.

I didn't think anyone would believe me, then I realized that it wasn't important, what was important is that I followed my highest path and brought forward whatever arose for me to grapple with...pure ceremony. How fun is that?

Once that decision was made, this whole 10 year mission to help Bill Long heal and move into the light started and led to Etta, then Tom McCarty and on to the others. Unbelievable but true. Now, this is really living life to the fullest from my perspective. To stare down the unbelievable and embrace the probable possibilities, backing it all up with real life science and data. The best of all worlds opened before me. So let's get on with it.

Know that the "Frank Smith alias The Sundance Kid" story has as many twists and turns, DNA revelations we didn't want to know because it meant back to the drawing board, and challenges as did Bill Long's. Once I had solid ground proof that Bill Long was indeed William Henry Long, alias The Sundance Kid, then I turned my attentions back to Frank Smith.

Frank's wife Julia Etta's story was much easier to discover. MEGA POLYGAMIST FAMILIES have their strengths when one wants to research. They have a huge amount of genealogy and family histories already written and available to make your journey much easier.

In fact, without this, the passion for genealogy and family history the MEGA POLYGAMIST FAMILES have, this story would not have been possible.

Moving forward...In search of the illusive Etta, female outlaw who rode with Butch and Sundance, I added research about her to my schedule when her spirit came to me in the middle of the night, 3 am to be exact, and she said, "You must help me, my children are killing themselves and if they knew who they were, they wouldn't do that."

Astounded, I reeled and rocked spiritually, trying to grasp what had just happened. Of course, I was excited to be able to help her, however challenging the ride.

YDNA of Bill Long's Bones and the Utah Cousins

60,000 Utah cousins. That's a lot of cousins and that's how many it took to prove the real identity of William Henry Long.

The mission I chose was focused on gathering massive amounts of data any way I could and process out of this data what happened to Bill Long's family and find his two sisters in the picture that he used to hang on the wall.

The focus in the beginning was proving The Sundance Kid alias William Henry Long was indeed Harry Longabaugh. My research and scientific YDNA samples shows he is not.

Bill Long is a Long according to his own YDNA. After 1,000 hours of genealogy research coupled with digging up second great grandfather's remains which to this day I hold extremely sacred calling that he asked me to help him heal and move into the light and this was the best way to do so.

This especially included a YDNA test for bones from Sorenson Genetics which was the first one done by them on the bones we just happened to have in their lab at the exact time they needed some bones to do their new test. A $10,000 gift for free.

That was wonderful, except Bill Long's Y DNA said NOT A MATCH. WOW, I was not prepared for that, but it is so. Science came through with Y DNA and MITO DNA.

You cannot please everyone and on the Outlaw Trail, you usually can't please anyone. And most of the time they just want a shoot-out. However, I am comforted by the words of James Taylor, "Shower the people you love with love, show them the way that you feel. Things will be much better if you only will."

I was so disappointed that I could not help Uncle Jerry prove that Bill Long was Harry Longabaugh that I gave up the quest, disillusioned, depressed, the wind had completely gone out of my sails. I was despondent that we may never find Bill's Long's sisters.

Well, after giving up on the Outlaw Trail Adventure as I wanted it to be, I resigned. Done with Ancestry.com, done with driving all night to meet obscure people in obscure places explaining to them the wild adventure I was on and why I needed their family history and often their DNA swab for comparisons.

Finding these people and getting swabs was a lot of hard work and sometimes I didn't want to do what needed to be done. I learned to do it, then I learned to get excited about it, but it was arduous. So, I was done with it!

Until...my brother, D. Ross Nickle, got another adventure to ride for and back on the Outlaw Trail we rode. Our grandmother, Luzernia Jackson (Nickle, Baker) played with Vindie, the youngest daughter of Bill and Luzernia. Though Vindie was a few years older, they lived next door and were playmates there in Fremont, Wayne County, Utah.

We went back to the drawing boards and family lore and found some very strong indications that The Sundance Kid alias William Henry Long was actually Tom McCarty (if you asked me) or Bill McCarty his brother (if you ask my brother D. Ross Nickle).

Back to Ancestry.com and McCarty family genealogy and family histories and the search for live descendants. That's not an easy task.

The McCarty family is a great family and I have enjoyed the 4 years I have been researching their family fully believing The Sundance Kid alias William Henry Long was a McCarty.

I felt especially attracted to this theory from the family story told by Bill Long himself, that he and his son were in a robbery and his son was killed. My take on that now says Bill Long rode with the McCarty's and was hanging back at the base camp or some significant part of the relay when Bill McCarty's son was killed.

So how did Bill Long come to know the McCarty's? Bill Long was 16 in 1880 the year he mother died. He lived 7 miles from Lewiston, Idaho in Asotin, Washington, where the only building left standing is a church.

My conjecture is as follows: Bill Long met up with the McCarty's in Baker, Oregon area and his training began. Bill's brother, Nelson Long, spent time in the penitentiary for stealing a horse. Evidences that Bill may have been drawn to the outlaw side of life fairly early on.

The Boys From Illinois

Here's a good time to introduce the "Illinois Boys". Bill Long came out of Illinois, Wyatt Earp as well, Abraham Lincoln was of course an Illinois boy and the list goes on. The political climate of Illinois was front and center to the progress of settling America.

Wyatt Earp, by the way, at the end of his life went to San Bernardino, California, area and started a saloon. The next town down the road there was another saloon that was owned and ran by one Ellis Eames, the same Ellis Eames who is grandfather to Etta. And they were all there in San Bernardino, California the same time that the Younger Family came through.

Introducing the MEGA Polygamist Families

This Ellis Eames was the grandfather to Etta. The first Etta whom Butch fell in love with in Milford, Utah. He was also half owner of Hahn's Mill on the Shoal River in Missouri.

As the 250 armed men sent by Governor Boggs of Missouri to exterminate the Mormons massacred the Mormons at Hahn's Mill, Ellis Eames barely escaped into the dark woods. He had a bullet hole in his coat tails but was alive along with his first wife and children.

He was a polygamist, not yet but would be once he became the first mayor of Provo, Utah, under the guidance of Brigham Young. He and his young family hid in the cold, damp woods and somehow survived the terrifying night when many of their friends, neighbors and family members were massacred and horribly so.

They survived, came out west, settled in Utah Valley and when the call came for saints to go settle a sea port for Brigham Young in 1852, Ellis Eames and his family were first in line.

Alias MODOC BILL of Deadwood

Deadwood, South Dakota, was another wild and ferocious mining town that would eat you up, spit you out and laugh at you. According to Wikipedia, "The illegal settlement of Deadwood began in the 1870s on the territory granted to **American Indians** in the 1868 **Treaty of Laramie**.

The treaty had guaranteed ownership of the **Black Hills** to the **Lakota people**, and disputes over the Hills were ongoing, having

13

reached the **United States Supreme Court** on several occasions.

However, in 1874, Colonel **George Armstrong Custer** led an expedition into the Hills and announced the discovery of gold on French Creek near present-day **Custer**, South Dakota. Custer's announcement triggered the **Black Hills Gold Rush** and gave rise to the lawless town of Deadwood, which quickly reached a population of around 5,000.

According to the official records of Deadwood, the road agents of 1870's record one Bill Long who's alias was MODOC BILL. He hung out with Texas Charlie.

Bill at the time was a horse thief. This same Bill Long is likely the same William Henry Long that married my second great grandmother, Luzernia and went on to take on the name of The Sundance Kid.

Now, another evidence of this comes from the history of the Willamette Valley, Clackamas City to be exact. William Henry Long alias MODOC BILL, alias The Sundance Kid, no doubt spent time with his father James Long and his new step-mother Louisiana Baldwin Long in Clackamas City area of what is now known as Portland, Oregon.

The most resilient of Indian tribes, the Modoc Indians, cost the US Government over 1 million dollars to capture and annihilate all but 400 of them. They were led by one Captain Jack who successfully led his people and are famous for being the last Indian tribe to fall under the practices of genocide and annihilation being used by the territorial governments under the direction of the US Government.

They were tough and resilient, smart and wise. It cost more to take the Modoc Indians down that any other tribe.

They were in the same area that William Henry Long was in, the Willamette Valley and the surrounding country. Bill Long would have been well aware of their fierce fight for preserving their people, their land and their way of life. He obviously had deep and abiding respect for their abilities by his use of MODOC BILL while in the Deadwood, South Dakota area.

Deadwood 1876, The Sundance Kid alias MODOC Bill alias of William Henry Long, Butch Cassidy, Robber's Roost in Wayne County, Utah.

CHAPTER 2

The Bloody Watch on Boulder Mountain

"Shots from a long rifle screamed through the quite morning air in Delta, Colorado. First one, a minute pause, and then the second deadly shot found its mark. A bloody scene and two McCarty's were dead." This was in Delta, Colorado on the 3rd day of September in 1893. Mr. Stimpson, however of the local hardware store, had a dream the night before that someone robbed his hardware store, across the street from the Bank in Delta.

Stimpson was ready with a loaded rifle even though it was against the law to carry a loaded rifle in Delta, Colorado in 1893. He was also a sharp shooter from his days in the army. When he heard shots cracking through the morning air coming from the bank, he ran out into the street, knelt down, aimed an waited a moment for the horses to come out of the alley.

Crack, a shot rang out and Bill McCarty fell from his horse never to move again. Stimpson ran the half block to the alley where the other two McCarty's were making their escape. When Bill's son turned to see his father, another shot rang out and both father and son were dead. It was 10:35 am when the shots were fired at the McCarty's.

This leaves Tom McCarty making his escape leaving his nephew and his brother dead in the streets of Delta, Colorado on the 7th day of

September in 1893. They were buried outside the cemetery up on the hill where their graves are still located though they are now inside the cemetery boundaries, cemeteries expanding as they do over the years.

More evidences from Grandpa Sundance and his connection to the McCarty's came from a bloody watch that was found at the 9,000 foot level on Boulder Mountain, Wayne County,Utah. I found very strong evidences on that mountain that Tom McCarty spent from September 10th September 26th in a half cabin.

There's a likelihood Bill Long was a part of this due to the timing, the location and the story that Luzernia brought Bill Long in from the desert twice. Once in 1891 and once in 1893. September 26, 1893, was the day that Silas Morrell, her husband died and that's also the last date on the trees recorded on Boulder Mountain at the bloody watch site.

The Canyon Cowboy, my great uncle Perry Jackson, knew Bill Long very well. It was a 9 year old Perry who went to show Grandpa Bill that he could shoot his pistol. Grandpa said that was mighty fine shooting, except you would likely get yourself killed shooting like that, point, aim, shoot.

"You didn't have time for aiming like that in a real gun fight," said Grandpa Sundance. Bill showed him how to run his pointing finger along the barrel and shoot with his 3rd finger on the trigger. "When you want to shoot, point and shoot, like this…it's much faster." Uncle Perry was astounded and remembered those lessons with Grandpa Long. They were like no one else's.

That 9 year old grandson grew up, grew old and died as the cycle of life goes. At Great Uncle Perry's funeral, we met a cousin of a cousin who had found a bloody watch up on the Aquarian Plateau. My Outlaw Trial Adventure partner (who doubles as my brother) D. Ross Nickle, and I were up on Bolder Mountain by that afternoon. It took us two trip to finally find the site.

I instinctively knew we needed to find writing on the trees. I had seen an article about Butch and the Boys leaving signs on trees to communicate with each other. I was sure there were signs here somewhere. It was a large grove of trees on a huge mountain of aspens. Finding the one we needed was a bit of a chore.

Especially since we didn't know there were signs, I had dreamed about there being writing carved on the trees, my intuition told me they were there…keep looking. But I'm not 100% accurate; no one I know is, so it's an act of courage and dedication to check out your instincts under this circumstance. But stay we did and viola...

For two hours we braved the mountain terrain through the quakies thick with mosquitoes until we could stand no more and were on our way back to the original watch site when I looked up and saw JTM in the most beautiful cursive carved into a 100 year old aspen. Astounding as it was, there the initials of John Thomas McCarty were on the tree.

I looked some more and found the tale-tell date 9/10/93. This was 3 days after the Delta, Colorado bank robbery. This watch had blood on it. The clock hands stopped at 10:35, which was 5 minutes after the Delta Bank Robbery. There was a bullet indentation on the case.

It was astounding, an unbelievably awesome find. This was the place where Tom McCarty stayed until the coast was clear and he could leave once again. After the Delta, Colorado back robber on September 7, 1893, Tom McCarty hid here in a half height, make-shift cabin and carved dates on the trees and his initials. I believe Bill Long was there also. He was likely part of the first camp just outside of Delta, Colorado or some connection of significance in this story.

The whole reason we believed that William Henry Long was a McCarty stemmed from family stories about the family saying he stopped robbing banks after his son was killed. Now, this could also have been added family stories after people read the books about the McCarty's.

As the day wore on and our explorations in search of the tree inscriptions from over 100 years ago alluded for over 2 hours, my brother said, "You know, Sis, I'm done with looking for inscriptions of trees, I'm going back to searching the area of the watch and the cans."

However disappointed I was, I knew the mosquito's thick as a blanket in the sweltering hot afternoon that he efforts were a great gift looking for something his sister wanted to find. As we walked back to look where he wanted to look, I was following my brother.

Still looking at every tree, yet I was losing hope of finding anything so I wasn't so adamant or careful about my search. It was just a great hope that I would see something as a last ditch effort on my way to doing another search.

We spoke of how unlikely is was that even if the trees existed 100 years ago, aspens have a life span of less than a hundred years. At best we were stretching this envelope. Having reasoned our way out of further exploration efforts in the aspens, I looked over my left shoulder just above eye height and there were the initials JTM.

It was large, stylized, the most beautiful initials I've ever seen on a carved tree. In fact the initials were so well done that it's rare to find handwriting on regular paper so finely written. My eyes had to focus three times before my mind could catch up with the treasure I had just found. Ross! Ross! I was hollering and my brother was right there. We decided this was probably what we were looking for. The initials of John Thomas McCarty.

Such a thrill, but there was hesitation when realized that more solid evidences to prove it was indeed John Thomas McCarty's initials were needed. All we had so far were strong evidences which were thrilling, but not strong enough to take to the world and make this claim…not yet.

I was so excited my whole body was trembling and my mind was racing. Back and forth, round and round, tree after tree after tree…such a remote chance that we would find anything else yet so hopeful. Ross found the next treasure. Not 30 feet from the JTR initials was another old aspen with the date 3/10/93.

Three days after the Delta Bank Robbery! "Holy Toledo," was all I could say. "Can you believe this bro?" finally replaced Holy Toledo. This was the verification we needed to prove this was indeed the site where John Thomas McCarty came after the Delta Bank Robbery.

And the piece of the McCarty puzzle came together. 4 years of McCarty research paid off. Did I mention that we met our cousin of cousins at Uncle Perry Jackson's funeral? Yes, my Great Uncle Perry Jackson died in his mid 90's after spending a life time steeped in Wayne County history and adventures. He was known as The Canyon Cowboy and actually spent time in Hollywood. It took several trips to make all the discoveries the site had to offer, so far this is what we have discovered:

- ❖ A bloody watch on Boulder Mountain
- ❖ An aspen with the initials JTM carved into it over 100 years ago
- ❖ JTM initials match the only know signature style of Tom McCarty in his wife's brother's journal page recording her death
- ❖ A Half-cabin, 10 feet square, that was often built for a short-term shelter
- ❖ Date of 10 Sep 1893 carved on another 100 year old aspen 30 feet from the initials
- ❖ Several dates throughout September, 1893, with the final date 26 Sep

- ❖ 26 Sep was the date Luzernia's husband, Silas Morrell died down in the valley below
- ❖ Bill Long knew Luzernia from 1891 when she saved his life
- ❖ Numerous cans pre-1915
- ❖ Site located near the main trail Escalante to Loa, Utah
- ❖ The hands on the watch were stopped at 10:35, 5 minutes after the Delta Bank Robbery began in Delta Colorado
- ❖ Bullet indentation on the watch which stopped the hands and 10:35 on that fateful day

Astounding as all of that is, I was committed to finding a signature of John Thomas McCarty. Finally after an exhausting internet search, I found his signature on the journal page of his wife, Teenie's record of death. Her brother, a Christiansen, recorded her death in his journal and Tom signed it at the bottom. The signature was an exact match to the letter JTM on the quaking aspen that was over 100 years old on top of the Aquarian Plateau near Boulder Mountain, Utah.

However, it's time to claim this as a substantial OUTLAW TRAIL SITE, found by one of my cousins, researched and explored by myself and my brother, D Ross Nickle.

It was these types of data and information that led us to believe Bill Long was a McCarty. However, William Henry Long is not a McCarty according to Y DNA testing.

The family lore says that Bill Long's son's death in a robbery, made Bill decide to quit his outlaw ways. I'm still curious about this family story because in the end the DNA both MITO DNA and Y DNA came up a NO MATCH. The Sundance Kid alias McCarty was NOT A MATCH. We're still open for information about a robbery where a son of Bill's was hot; this story is still in a possibility, but I now believe it was the Bill McCarty and his son's death on 7 Sep 1893.

Again, I believe William Henry Long ran with the McCarty's upon occasion, and was on the backup team in the camp outside Delta, Colorado when Tom McCarty, the lone surviving McCarty, came riding in full steam, changed horses, and rode for their lives. 3 days later they were on the Aquarian Plateau between Escalante and Loa, Wayne County, Utah.

The bloody watch my cousin of cousins found at 9,000 near the quakies with the date 3/10/93 carved on the tree verify this as a substantial Outlaw Site. I believe this site was chosen because it was above Loa, Wayne County, Utah where Luzernia was. She was my second great grandmother and she had saved Bill Long's life once before in the "Muddy Dubb" are below Rico, Colorado on the Deloris River.

The family lore says that Luzernia went out into the desert two times to save Bill. I believe this was the second time. And the timing is fascinating. Silas Morrell, Luzernia's husband, died that same month. Silas died on the 26th of September 1893. That date is the last date on the aspen trees up on the Aquarian Plateau Outlaw Site we call "Bloody Watch on Bolder Mountain."

When the DNA testing between Bill Long and Tom McCarty came up a "NO MATCH" I was stunned. This was a huge disappointment and so confusing that I was totally overwhelmed and gave up the Outlaw Trail Adventure for good, this time for sure.

If Bill Long wanted to move into the light he would have to help me a lot more than it seemed had been done up until that conclusion that he was not a McCarty. So much time, energy and money had gone into this that if you said the O word (outlaw) I would run the other way. I was good moving on. Until a few days later…I felt the call to Ride on another Outlaw Trail Adventure.

Outlaw Trail Adventures, Genealogy Database, OTAGD

This is precisely why The Outlaw Trail Genealogy Database became so strategic and the center to my story. It kept revealing secrets and tales based on genealogy facts, census records, births, deaths, family histories. (Oh my goodness, do polygamist families love to tell their stories and do their genealogy. Thank you so very much, my ancestors, I honor you.)

In fact, this is another part of the symbiotic relationship between Outlaws and Polygamists, their genealogy revealing the places they lived, the people there were related to, and showed how highly significant these MEGA POLYGAMIST FAMILIES were to our tales here on The Outlaw Trail.

About this time, I was so torn between what I was experiencing and how I was going to tell the story. The research took all the time, energy and money I had and writing an Outlaw Book just wasn't calling to me.

Many, many people out there are die hard outlaw adventure dedicated enthusiasts. Some very articulate and most very knowledgeable about every robbery, etc, that I was overwhelmed and decided my time was up.

I was never going to achieve that level of sophistication in the outlaw world. It just wasn't my inclination, it didn't call to me. Yet, here I was on the outlaw trail and really felt compelled to write my story and the stories of my adventures…then all of a sudden the whole chaotic conflicted confusions ceased in my mind and I knew what called to me exactly. I was going to write about the Ghost Riders of the Wild Bunch.

Since this time, however, I met a Utah cousin of mine, Steve DeFriez, from Castle Dale, Utah. He's my 6th cousin on the Allred lines, but Allred cousins generally love family histories and cousins. Come to find out, he knew the northern half of the San Rafael Swell as well as I knew the southern half.

AND his grandfather, Paul Hansen, Polley as he was called, met Butch Cassidy at Swasey's Leap while Butch was training his horses to jump the leap. Polly was 17 at the time, a tall, blond handsome Dane herding 3,000 head of sheep in the Head of Sinbad area.

On the day of the Castle Gate Robbery, well the day after to be exact, Butch Cassidy, Elza Lay and Bub Meeks jumped the leap and spent 3 days with Polley Hansen helping him move his 3,000 head of sheep and doing a little horse trading.

Historical Geocaching was born out of our union. If you go to www.outlawtrailadventures.com or outlawtrailadventures on Facebook you can get in on taking the adventure with a 12 hour geocache run called "The Escape From Castel Gate".

My amazing Utah cousins and friends in Emery County had a wealth of information which we put together and geocached for you so you can take the adventure ourselves. Ride where Butch rode and experience Butch Cassidy's Escape from Castle Gate for yourselves.

Now back to our story.

A huge relief seized my mind and then my body and I was totally joyful. Remember, I'm a psychic medium by nature. This is my story, my experiences and my desires to write about my spiritual adventures in such a way that others coming along might learn, expand and thoroughly enjoy my adventures.

This was the way I had been looking for. Writing MY Ghost Story was so clear, so simple, so me and in perfect alignment with my chosen mission in life. How very exciting was that set of epiphanies! Huge waves of gratitude filled my mind, body and spirit.

This will have meaning to only a few of you out there. The cleric minded and the spiritual path minded. It's all good. I just wanted to claim this adventure and be true to my passions and heart's desires on my highest life path. My Optimal Life Trajectory as the Remote Viewers of the world would describe it.

Speaking of the Profound; one of the most profound secrets revealed itself to me quite by accident, at least that's what it look like from my perspective at the time. I was looking up data about my second great grandmother, Luzernia Ann Allred (Morrell, Long) who married The Sundance Kid alias William Henry Long (after saving his life in Colorado). I found the first census she showed up in. It was 1860 in Fort Ephraim.

Whoa, that was a shock. Then research revealed that the Allred Clan led by James Allred, grandfather to Luzernia Ann or "Zernie" as she was called, started out in Fort Harmony down just north of St. George across the highway from Kolob Canyon.

Why we care about this is John D. Lee (who's 4th great grandson was a childhood friend of mine) of the Mountain Meadow Massacre fame, live in the same fort. James Allred reports that, "John D Lee didn't think he needed any counselors," speaking of the leadership in the Mormon Church in southern Utah. They live together for about 7 years when James Allred moved his family to Spring City, Utah.

The Sand Box at Fort Ephraim 1860, "The Baby Bunch"

What incredible stories that unfolded before my eyes when I pushed the enter key and saw Fort Ephraim census 1860. It was what I call "The Baby Bunch." So isn't your curiosity perked just a tad bit? Can't you just see these little 3 year olds and other kids sitting in the sand box at Fort Ephraim? It was a war zone at that point; the Black Hawk Indian War was raging.

So who was playing in the sand box at Fort Ephraim? Luzernia Ann Allred, 3 year old daughter of Andrew Jackson Allred and Chloe Stevens. She was the future wife to first Silas Morrell and then when Silas died, she was wife to The Sundance Kid alias William Henry Long. Next to her was a 3 year old named Teenie Christiansen.

Both were daughters of polygamists. Teenie was sister to one Willard Christiansen (yet to be born) who became known as Matt Warner, who would become the brother-in-law to Tom McCarty. Matt

Warner was one of the Invincible Three along with Butch Cassidy and Tom McCarty.

The three of them left Wyoming being chased by the Cheyenne Social Club, the Cattleman's Association lead by the governor, in a "rain of bullets", barely escaping with their lives. All of this means Teenie, who grew up for a period of time playing in the sandbox at Fort Ephraim with Zernie, grew up to marry none other than Tom McCarty. Speaking of Tom, he would have come to the fort for trading purposes because he lived nearby in a town called Levan.

Interesting to watch how the web of life is weaved.

Outlaw Camp Sites

Introducing one of the delightful discoveries I was fortunate enough to experience on The Outlaw Trail: Outlaw Camp Sites. There are Cowboy Camp Sites out there and they all have old cans, pre-1915 because there's a small center made of lead in the top of each can. Post 1916 they changed the canning process. Outlaw Camp Sites have a distinctly different ambience: about half the cans are flasks, whiskey flasks. Interesting, Interesting.

CHAPTER 3

Meeting Etta's Ghost
& Etta's Utah Cousins

"Don't spend much time on this one, it's probably nothing."
When my brother said this, I knew it was time to research.

I opened my trusty Outlaw Trail Adventures Genealogy
Database. The first round of investigations showed this was not the
Etta I was looking for. Another huge disappointment after all that
research.

Upon giving up, I cried. I was so sure I was right and it would
have been a lot of fun finding the real Etta. Having some of the
finest genealogy I've ever encountered telling me Etta mother's
genealogy was certainly solid looking. I showed she was not the
Etta we thought she might be.

Then, in frustration at having reached yet another dead end,
with my bored fingers on the keyboard basically doodling, the
intuitive hit that says, "What if this genealogy is wrong? What if
that's not the right mother?"

"What? Are you nuts? This is the best genealogy I've ever
seen," I said vehemently. The inkling came again, "Look beyond
this information, keep looking, this is not the mother you are
looking for."

Ugh! Exasperated yet intrigued I looked further. Four hours later, at 3 am, I came across the real mother for our Etta. Ellen Sophia Jacobs. The right Ellen Sophia and there she was. With a little hunting and pecking, it became clear this was in fact the right mother for our Etta.

The incredible possibilities blew my mind and this began the double mystery research phase. If you think one mysterious outlaw is fun, try two or three. But I made a promise to my ghost and I was determined to keep that promise.

Somewhere along in here, while researching Etta's family, she came to me in the night and said, "Please help me. My children are killing themselves and if they knew who they were, they would quit doing that."

WOW! Of course I said yes, but it blew my mind. I had a hard time believing it, never mind telling anyone else.

As I researched and researched, did site discoveries, found live descendants, the story began to unfold and low and behold, this Etta was related by marriage to The Sundance Kid! Yes, The Sundance Kid alias William Henry Long. Now what to do with her husband, Frank E Smith. Frank Smith was one of the aliases for The Sundance Kid. See Wikipedia.

Clue Number 1: her birth certificate said her name was Julietta yet her head stone said Julia **Etta** Smith. Once I saw this possibility that Julietta changed how her name was put together by the time she died to Julia Etta, I was thrilled.

I didn't know for sure yet, but I got in my little Saturn II and drove through the night through a snow storm to get to the Price Cemetery where she was buried. I couldn't wait any long.

If her name on her head stone said Julia Etta, I was sure she was the Etta that danced with Butch Cassidy in 1892 through 1894 out of Milford, Utah.

Digging down through 8 inches of snow on her head stone…Julia…drum roll…space…drum roll…and there it was, Etta.

Astonished I was reeling and shaking my head in remarkable belief through my disbelief. This was the first great clue, well, no. It was the second great clue.

The first great clue blew me right out of the water. It takes literally thousands of hours to build The Outlaw Trail Genealogy

Database. And it's still in research mode and evolving. However, the rich treasures contained therein and the ones I haven't yet discovered through those Utah Cousins and their family trees winding through the westward immigration from the founding fathers of America and beyond.

So, when I was given the name of Julia Ames I began to go digging. Ancestry.com is filled with countless man hours of dedicated genealogists, family historians and others who have gifted their work to the collective that all might benefit there from.

My beloved angel mother was one of these great women and men. She spent years researching, typing on an old Selectric typewriter, filling binders with family group sheets and pedigree charts telling remarkable history after interesting history. I honor these people, every single one of you. Without you I could not have put this story together.

I begin a new family tree with Julia Ames and her husband Frank E. Smith. The information was sketchy at first. Everything the family had shared with me was helpful but stopped at Frank E. Smith and his wife Julia.

Then we found family, remember the woman who was supposed to be dead and was supposed to have lived in Payson? She was very much alive and living in Hanksville, Utah and she had the genealogy for Julia which gave us the breakthrough we were looking for on her lines.

Her mother's name was Ellen Sophia Jacobs. Her father was George Monteville Ames whose father was Ellis Eames, the first mayor of Provo, Utah. Truly thrilling to find fascinating mysteries to add to the ones you already have.

Etta's grandfather was a mystery man, different members of the family had different perspectives on whether they want to know about him or not. There were a few questionable issues. One last test and it all proved out. I had found her real mother and all the family genealogy you could ever want. And her great aunt by marriage was married to the Prophet Joseph Smith, just for interest sake. Add to that, her great uncle, Lot Huntington, was a Danite and had a group that followed him.

The people of Utah had no reason to trust the US Government and by 1862 there was resistance to a governor being installed. Brigham Young was their undisputed leader, Prophet and Governor. It became so heated that Lot Huntington was shot by Orrin Porter Rockwell at Camp Floyd in 1862 for his part in the fiasco. Lot's "Gang" of Danites surrendered. There is so much…be patient, all in due time. The family history is rich and full in fascinating connections. Off I went and another Outlaw Trail Adventure. Lot Huntington is Etta's Great Uncle.

Meet the Ghost of Etta's Real Mother, Ellen Sophia

Also in the sandbox in 1860 at Fort Ephraim, was another 3 year old name Ellen Sophia Jacobs, mother to Etta. She was the one who kept telling me (MEET THE GHOST OF ETTA'S MOTHER) her genealogy on Ancestry.com was incorrect and it was strategically significant to figure out who she really was and who her family really was. "Ignore the pretty work" and get the real stuff, find her, "I'm a Utah girl," she said.

I did what she guided me to do, and amazing mysteries began to resolve out of the massive data on Ancestry.com.

How The Wild Bunch is related, each of them is critical to understanding our tales, and the latest revelation told us of Etta's great uncle, Lot Huntington, being shot in 1862 by Orrin Porter Rockwell at Camp Floyd. Lot Huntington was a Danite and the leader of a gang according to the information at Camp Floyd.

This discovery came this month, July 2014 when I went to a paranormal conference ghost hunt at Camp Floyd. The email announcing it jumped out of my computer while I was looking for something else.

Meet more of the people who are key players in our story, so you can keep up with the unfolding and appreciate the significance of the parts they played.

More Exciting Ghosts to Meet and Greet on Outlaw Trail Adventures

1. **Andrew Jackson Allred,** (my 3rd great grandfather) son of James Allred who settled first in Fort Harmony with John D Lee and the on the Spring City, Utah. At the age of 16, "Jack Allred" as he was called, rode in the wagon train across the plains with Brigham Young. At Jack's Point near between Fremont and Loa in Wayne County, he built a trading post and had a saw mill there on the Fremont River. He ran the mail up over Fish Lake

Mountain. Mail runners before him and been killed by the Indians on Fish Lake Mountain. He took the time to learn the Indian language and knew how to speak effectively with the Indians and was a great leader. Jack Allred was living in Spring City and had married Chloe Stevens with whom he had children. One of his children was Luzernia Ann Allred or "Zernie".
By 1894 Zernie's first husband, Silas Morrell had died and she married The Sundance Kid alias William Henry Long, who saved the family farm on the East Bench in Rabbit Valley above Fremont. It was the only spread with the river running through the door step. He also was instrumental in saving the Dairy Farm up on Fish Lake Mountain by Silas Springs. Finally, Luzernia and her children never had to go without food again. Perfect hiding place.

2. **Ellis Eames**, Grandfather to Etta. He was the first mayor of Provo, Utah ended up a saloon owner in San Bernardino, California
    a. He was a great man who put himself on the line over and over to build, rebuild and make a better life for his family.
    b. Was half owner of Hahn's Mill and was there on 31 Oct 1948 when the massacre came upon them. His first of 3 wives was there and took their 4 little ones and hid in the forest. Ellis waved to them as he ran in a rain of bullets coming down upon him. Only one touched him at all and that one went through the tail of his suit coat.
    c. First mayor of Provo under the direction of Brigham Young. Took on 2 more wives, though he was somewhat resistant, he finally took it on.
    d. Went in early 1850's with the saints to settle a sea port in southern California. The settled 77,000 acres of what became known as San Bernardino, California, which they had purchased for 77,000 dollars.
    e. After 7 years, they were called home in 1857 when Johnston's army was at Fort Bridge, Wyoming, marching on Utah to squelch the Mormon rebellion.
    f. Ellis Eames sent his first two wives home to Payson to be with their families when he decided to leave the

church and started the RLDS church. He also started a saloon. Wyatt Earp was in the area just up the road with his own saloon.

g. When they came across the Mohave Desert on the way home (on their way they almost died of thirst in the desert) they also had difficulty with finding enough water.

h. Stayed in Beaver, Utah, in the winter of 1857-1858, on their way home. Not Ellis Eames, but his son, George Monteville Ames, father to Etta. He would have been 12 years old and had all winter to get to know the people in Beaver, Utah. Butch's grandfather, Robert Parker lived in Beaver at the time. Likely they knew each other. Maximillion Parker, Butch's father to be, would have been living in Beaver as well.

i. Thomas Coleman Younger, Cole Younger's family members were in the San Bernardino area at the time. Another fun story. He would have been there when Etta's father was there.

3. **Julietta Ames The first Etta that Butch Cassidy fell in love with in 1894 to 1896 in Milford, Utah.**

a. Born 1877, Payson, Utah

b. She was a very beautiful woman.

c. Changed name from Juliette Ames to Julia Etta (Ames) Smith on her head stone

d. 16 years old in Milford, Utah in 1894 and danced the night away with Butch Cassidy the Milford dances.

e. Was disowned by her father for it.

f. Met Frank Smith at the boarding house in Cove, Utah in 1896.

g. Was related to Butch Cassidy

h Fit much of the description of Etta exactly.

i. Married to Frank Smith. Frank Smith was one of the main aliases for The Sundance Kid.

j. She was 5'3" tall.

3. **Frank E. Smith**

a. Married to Etta (Julia Etta Ames (Smith))

b. Rode into Wayne County, Utah with Bill Long.

c. Married Julia Etta Ames in 1896 in Loa, Utah.

d. Lived with Julia Etta in Fish Creek late 1890's.

e. YDNA says he likely came out of the Netherlands where the Schmidt, Smith name did originate.

4. George Monteville Ames

a. Father to Etta (Julia Etta Ames (Smith))

b. Traveled to San Bernardino, California and returned at age 12 to Utah in 1897-1898 when Brigham Young recalled the saints under the treats of a Utah War with the US Government

c. Stayed in Beaver, Utah that winter

d. Lived next door to Luzernia and Bill Long inLyman, Wayne County, Utah

5. **Milford Bard Farnsworth**, brother-in-law to Julia Etta

    a. His nephew Cyrus Walter Farnsworth married Butch Cassidy's aunt Eva Clara Bentenson.

    b. Julia now has a direct relationship to Butch: she is his, well in-law through marriage; we'll get into the details as we go.

6. **Rosina Ames**, sister to Julia Etta Ames

    a. Grandma Tiny, both she and Etta were very tiny

    b. Lived in Price in later years, they called it "Little Hollywood"

c. She and her sister Julia were the children of George Monteville Ames and Ellen Sophia Flanders. Their mother died in childbirth with their younger sister after 11 days. This left baby Etta to be cared for by her aunt Sarah Elvira Flanders who married Samuel Meacham.

d. There was a wedding in Panguitch in 1892. Rosina married Milford Bard Farnsworth. It is very likely that Butch would have been at that wedding since they were in close proximity and a few years later Butch's Aunt Cyrus Walter Farnsworth and cemented in the relationships.

7. **William Ellsworth Lay**, while we're talking about outlaws of the Wild Bunch. One of the wildest places in the west at the time was Fort Ellsworth. I believe Elza used Ellsworth for that reason. This is my own opinion. Secondly, I believe the Lay family was out here in Utah though

I can't reconcile this with the Lay family genealogy, yet, but I haven't delved in deep...yet. That's another project

Lay family in Utah was directly tied to Julie Etta Ames (Smith) and her family. They had direct connections in Southern Utah and especially significant in San Bernardino, California. The final connector which is also a close and very significant one: Frank and Julie Etta Smith living in Hiawatha, Utah at the same time that Elza Lay had holdings in mining in Hiawatha, Utah. Around 1910.

8. **Ellen Sophia Jacobs**, mother to Julia Etta. Was sitting in the sandbox with the rest of the Baby Bunch members who would grow up and be significant connections to Butch Cassidy, The Sundance Kid, Matt Warner, But Meeks, Tom McCarty and Joshua Sweat. Ellen Sophia Jacobs and her Mother Ellen Sophia Flanders have tales to tale of polygamy, early Mormon Church who married who in which temple and how many wives does he have? The tapestry is being weaved, take a deep breath and let it flow.

9. **Ellen Sophia Flanders**, grandmother to Julia Etta
a. Married one Dimick Baker Huntington after her first husband Collins Eastman Flanders died.
b. Dimick B Huntington was the number one Indian interpreter for Brigham Young.
c. Her sister-in-law was sealed to the Prophet Joseph Smith by her brother Dimick in the Nauvoo Temple he was also a Danite. He was the father to Lot Huntington.
d. Dimick B Huntington was a major player in settling Utah in oh so many ways.
e. They had one son or he adopted a son or at least the son took on his last name.

10. **Lot Elisha Huntington**, son to Dimick B Huntington, great uncle-in-law to Etta. He was the leader of a Danite gang (one of 3 known Danite gangs, leaders of these gangs: Lot Huntington, Orrin Porter Rockwell and Bill Hickman, story for another day) and was killed by none other than Orrin Porter Rockwell out in Camp Floyd. In fact, tonight 6/21/2014, I'm going to a Ghost Hunt at The Old

Stagecoach Inn in Fairfield, near Camp Floyd. When he was killed there if was called Fort Crittenden.

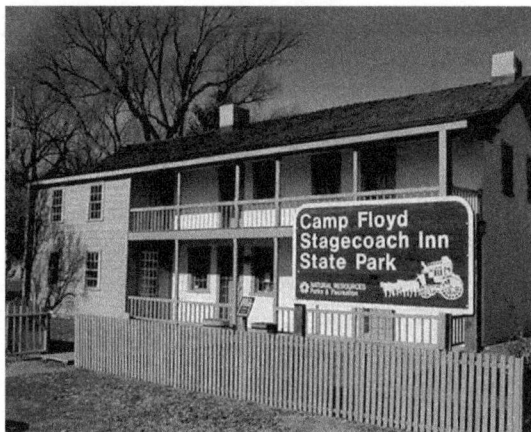

Description

This former military post quartered **the largest troop concentration in the United States from 1858 to 1861.** About 400 buildings housed the 3,500 troops sent West to suppress an assumed Mormon rebellion.

The troops returned East in 1861 for Civil War duty. Only a cemetery and commissary building remain as silent evidence of turbulent Camp Floyd.

Nearby Stagecoach Inn was an overnight stop on the historic overland stage and Pony Express route. The two-story adobe and frame hotel has been restored with original period furnishings. It is open daily from Easter weekend through October 15. The park is located 25 miles southwest of Lehi, Utah, on State Route 73.

Okay, Etta's great uncle was the leader of a Danite Gang who was killed by Orrin Porter Rockwell in 1862 at Camp Floyd. It's obvious the family that surrounded Julietta Ames, the name on her birth certificate, was deeply involved with the Mormon Church and its history. From Hahn's Mill to Camp Floyd, from Fort Ephraim to Cove Fort area near

Joseph, Utah. She had connections and each of these connections had impact as they do for all of us. Let's let history unfold before us.

So what do these people have to do with Etta and how do we get to the Sundance Kid alias William Henry Long? Etta and Bill Long are relatives through marriage and neighbors in Lyman and Fish Creek areas of Utah. In fact, Etta's sister was married to Walter Lazenby.

It seems that Bill Long's step-son Hiatt Morrell's wife, Ruby, had a mother who died when she was a teenager. Her father, Walter Lazenby, married Etta's sister.

Yes, indeed, in Fish Creek, Wayne County, Utah. Where the hell is Fish Creek? Google it, you might get lucky, near Teasdale, Utah in Wayne County. This is where The Sundance Kid alias Frank Smith lived in 1899. In fact, his first son, baby William Smith, is buried in the Lyman, Utah, cemetery just up the road.

Etta, or Julia Etta as she was known, and her husband of 50 years, Frank Edward Smith, had been living in Price, Utah for most of their adult lives. Their rich story spans a far distance and will be expanded upon in due time.

Since my involvement is all of this started with being asked to embark on the deepest of Sacred Journeys, that of helping another brother or sister to make the transition from the intense sadness and sorrow of living in shadow influence through the transition into making the frequency shifts to the Harmonic Convergence with Creative Intelligence. Simply put…heal and move into the light.

That's what Bill Long said the first night we met. And subsequently from him to Butch, Etta, Matt, Tom and Bill McCarty, Joshua Sweat, Bub Meeks, the Wild Bunch. It was totally unexpected on my part, but the rewards have been phenomenal.

CHAPTER 4

Free Flight Ceremony

Why in the world did I end up talking to a Ghost? And then promising him I would help him heal and move into the light? That's not the usual conversation one has with another, especially a ghost. Let me introduce a process of experiencing life which transforms my daily life into an amazing and astounding experience. This is process is what the Universe has guided me to do and what I have come to know as *Free Flight Ceremony*.

It began many, many moons ago. My heart's desire to experience a fullness of spirit, (unconditional love, sacred heart space) one where a powerful unfolding of streaming life experiences which was profound, life changing, regenerating, spontaneously healing, and self correcting.

In the very beginning of this, I just wanted to help my mother heal and feel better. She had been in pain with arthritis, lupus and related auto-immune system malfunctions and I really wanted to help her.

The traditional modern medicine options were helpful sometimes, did more harm than good other times. So, I began a journey in search of whatever I could find to help her in whatever ways were out there. Much of what unfolded before me as I grappled with life became honed down to a process which worked better than anything else I had experienced so far.

Again, spontaneously healing and self-correcting, that's how we are designed once we plug in and learn to step into the flow of the universe. AND so it is with the Creative Intelligence harmonizing with our intelligent natures is a **process I call Free Flight Ceremony on the Fabric of the Universe.** This is what I was seeking when I first felt the call to go to a full peyote ceremony with a Shaman named Don Andreas. It started oh so long ago, yet oh so recently.

It was not a recreational experience. It shook me up, tore me apart, turned me inside out, expanded me beyond anything I had ever imagined before. My consciousness journeyed far and wide and woke up on the Fabric of the Universe. Literally. It's not easy to explain but it's real.

And this creative intelligence which we are an intricate part of loves us enough to create us and let us play here having our life experiences to enrich and expand ourselves. It's our gift from a loving and powerful creative intelligence.

The ultimate gift was the understanding that anything I wanted to experience was given in the instant I wanted to experience it. The knowing that I woke up with was that life is actually like this with a few safety constraints to keep us alive while we learn to master our creative intelligence. Astounding.

Free Flight Ceremony is the most powerful spiritual tool I have ever experienced. Using Remote Viewing to find and process clear and accurate information and the applying Free Flight Ceremony, I have been able to accomplish astounding and fascinating things in supporting Bill Long's moving into the light which also goes hand in hand with my own spiritual evolution.

The following information explains how I use the gifts I have been given to help others and have the time of my life. That's just an awesome part of the gift. For those not on a transformational personal path just be patient for a page here. Thanks. Whether you find this boring, entertaining, insane or the most interesting page you've ever considered, let everyone have their experience. Just skip to the next page or two if you wish.

FREE FLIGHT UNIVERSE
WE ARE SELF EMPOWERED BY OUR VERY NATURE!

Everything you desire is within your reach in its highest form for you right now, connected to what is and empowered by your highest awareness. We are the most adventurous of the spiritual coaching teams on the planet.

You are the center of your universe, you are the core frequency and from this moment you can experience Your Exquisite Nature more and more with every breath...join us to this Ultimate Outcome as we do whatever it takes to meet and exceed the monsters eating you in your path and help you get on with what you came here to experience.

We're talking about nothing short of an Awakening, Ascension and the Ultimate Outcome of experiencing and living your Wholeness.

Take Back Control of Your Spiritual Wealth and tune up your Spiritual Health. Your physical form will thank you for it. When you are done with the shadow programming, look us up. When you are ready to break free of the conflict based paradigm, come see us. We are the shaman for the proverbial suburban shaman.

The ultimate mind/body/spirit reprogramming system is at your fingertips. You may have had your subconscious programming work against you in the past. With every piece of monster programming you have, you are being eaten. Bite by bite...That's what monsters do, they grow bigger and bigger every time you feed them monster fodder (thinking and feeling negative things) and then when you are ripe with shadow rising, they eat you. Now you can change that.

You have always had a choice. "With the Shadow Rising the Antidote" one of the most powerful mind/body/spirit reprogramming system available, your inner conscious mind and your conscious mind become supportive partners in creating your ultimate mind/body/spirit harmonics, which supports you on your spiritual path.

If you want to experience the universe in a new way through your sixth sense and beyond, if you desire to increase your ability to know when you are making the right choice in your life with more confidence and understanding, if you feel your soul calling you to stretch those wings of experience and find the next level for yourself, then give me a call and we'll facilitate the training for you. Find us at www.freeflightuniverse.com.

That's about it; just consider for a moment the following insights: If you have no Structure, you'll get lost. If you have no Focus, you'll get eaten by monsters. If you have no vision you'll get stuck.

Vision statement: Create structure from your passions, Focus with all your intensity and energies and live your visions by acting upon them thus making them real or finding something even better. Enjoy!

This is what I do, this is what I've spent my entire life training for and mastering. Again, I would stop at nothing because I wanted to help my mother and the people I love. My heart's greatest desire was to learn this and then share it.

It's pretty simple, really. A wee bit comprehensive, a great deal of fun, wild, risky, amazing, everything you could want to experience is on this path. The only challenge and I mean the ONLY CHALLENGE between you and this PATH are you "unfinished business", blocked and stuck energies.

As soon as you add the life giving energy of love and light you begin to spontaneously heal and self-correct. There is a process to this. Occasionally, it all comes complete, but usually it is a process. So again, welcome to my world and now you can begin to see how The Ghost of the Sundance Kid came to contact me. I was listening and willing to help. Most people aren't and don't. It's all as it should be, I'm really grateful that I was listening and that my basic nature is to help where I can be effective.

We now return to my spiritual journey. I had been adventuring into the intuitive realms with a very specific intention: accessing spiritual realms and bring manifestation into the physical realms...reality as we know it. And I really wanted it to be astounding and powerful to learn about what I did and the really significant things I was to bring through from intuitive realms.

In "17 Miracles", a movie about the most desperate and profound of the Mormon Treks across this great continent is captured and embodied in such a manner as to being us to tears with compassion and appreciation for our roots and all it took to get us to Utah. The rescuing parties: Ephraim Hanks first to find them, then Reddick Allred with his wagon and supplies to bring them back to the valley.

Regardless of your opinion about religion in general and Mormons is particular, what my people accomplished was often bordering on super human. But, pay attention to the time period, the dress, the mannerisms because this is the time in history that Butch Cassidy, Sundance, Etta and the rest were born and lived. There's a lot of rich history there and Ephraim Hanks is a Utah Cousin of ours.

The people he saved are Utah Cousins of ours. Hanksville, Wayne County, Utah was center field in our Outlaw Trail Adventures. Charley Gibbons had a store in Hanksville. Supplies from Charlie Gibbon's Store supplied Robbers Roost. I know, my second great grandmother, Zernie, worked for Charlie Gibbons in 1892 and took supplies into Robber's Roost upon occasion. You know her, she's the one who married William Henry Long alias The Sundance Kid.

The best definition of what I do is:

RATIONAL MYSTICISM

ra·tion·al *adjective*

1. 1.based on or in accordance with reason or logic.
   "I'm sure there's a perfectly rational explanation"

syno
nyms
:
  logical, reasoned, sensible, reasonable, cogent, intelligent, ju dicious, shrewd,commonsense, commonsensical, sound, prudent;

Definition of MYSTICISM

1. *1*: the experience of mystical union or direct communion with ultimate reality reported by mystics
2. *2*: the belief that direct knowledge of God, spiritual truth, or ultimate reality can be attained through subjective experience (as intuition or insight)

Now let's put the two together:

Rational mysticism, which encompasses both rationalism and mysticism, is a term used by scholars, researchers, and other intellectuals, some of whom engage in studies of how altered states of consciousness or transcendence such as trance, visions, and prayer occur. Lines of investigation include historical and philosophicalinquiry as well as scientific inquiry within such fields as neurophysiology and psychology.

Since I was able to consider for myself, I have practiced my own version of rational mysticism. As an adult, I acquired the skill of Remote Viewing spending 10 years honing my skills and I still am expanding m abilities in this arena.

The Cognitive Sciences Laboratory at Stanford University has scientifically proven its existence and viability. The government Remote Viewers provided over 30 years of scientifically based psychic viewing, Remote Viewing, data of all types.

It is these skills that brought about finding much of the information in this book...at least the key pieces coupled with extensive intellectual consideration, research and site work. I did my due diligence and these is my remarkable findings.

Experiments In Remote Viewing For Yourself: Just because you can, do the experiment for yourself. Have someone else choose a target, a verifiable target like a picture from a magazine. Have them put it in a folder and not let you see it.

Now just draw and write and doodle to your heart's content and when you are done, look to see if you were accurate at all. Joe McMoneagle, one of the government remote viewers, wrote a book called, "Remote Viewing." I highly suggest it if you want to know more.

I will be developing a course soon so keep you eyes on my web page and Facebook pages: www.outlawtrailadventures.com.

Chapter 5

William Henry Long, His True Identity

Back to Utah and settling the west. If the weather and nature weren't after you, the cattlemen were. The wealth of this period of time was cattle. Follow the money to understand the challenges. If the cattlemen weren't after you, the Indians were. If the Indians weren't after you the US government was sending Johnston's army after you. This were the facts of life in the Utah Territory in 1857.

And if that wasn't enough, the railroad and bankers were more favorable to the big business and money makers which is how business works and that's always good when business is working for everyone benefits with business is thriving.

Thriving businesses were generated mostly by the Thriving Patriarchs of the time, most of whom were MEGA POLYGAMISTS. When you want to settle a place like the West in the 1840's through 1900, you need Thriving Patriarch's and Matriarch's who can get the job done. But the federal government considered the Mormons as rebellious and from their perspective there may have been some unruliness out here in the Territory of Deseret.

Now to thicken the pot and add intensity of feelings and loyalties to Brigham Young and the Utah Cousins, add to the mix of challenges the "Federalies" coming after your fathers and grandfathers, and eventually your mothers and grandmothers for cohabitation (polygamy).

If they were convicted, they were put in deplorable and horrific conditions in Sugarhouse Prison across from the old Irving School that has been transformed into a condominium complex in the middle of Sugar House, Salt Lake County, Utah.

Hence, this is a story about Ghosts, Outlaws, Polygamists and DNA. This is my grand heritage, this is my heart and soul, this is my honor to Ride the Outlaw Trail through real life as seen through those who risked all and blazed the trails to Utah. I bring all I've learned forward that we might be edified, strengthened, humored and enjoyed.

If I inadvertently step on your toes, I apologize. This is the only way I could figure out to tell the whole story and it had to be told my way, to the best of my ability to tell.

On Solid Ground

Heads spinning, denial glaring, intellects flaring, that's where some of you are. I know you. That's right where you should be. I honor your position while I move forward to honor mine. They are not exclusive by any means and inclusive understand of things greater than we are leads to remarkable results.

Remote Viewing is my first love of intuitive skills and tools with which to experience the fullness of the Universe. I love it so because it provides clear and accurate feedback to concrete comparisons (for most views) and there's a very powerful and significant feedback loop between the left brain and the right brain. This facilitates the phenomenal learning curve that happens when one is doing remote viewing.

Welcome to my world. Remote Viewing protocol provides the powerful structure from which I gather intuitive data which provides added sources and information to the rest of my research and spiritual guidance.

Without immediate and powerful action being taken to implement the process of comparing and scoring data to known targets, you can get very good. If you have natural abilities inherent in your psyche and practice great things can come of your work. And this is what I have done. Did I mention it was really fun? I won't do anything unless it's fun.

My favorite experience on the outlaw trail gathering intuitive data and having to immediately useful was the time when someone had given me a name, Julia Ames. "Don't spend much time on it through, it's probably nothing," they said. And then find them where I felt prompted to look. Usually about 3 am was my best time to find really cool data.

As my research progressed I found a live descendent of Julia's who

42

was supposed to be living in Payson, Utah and was supposed to have a lot of valuable information on Julia and her husband Frank Smith. So I looked for her. And I looked, and looked some more.

No one by that name ever lived in Payson or at least had any public records in Payson and they certainly didn't die there and most certainly wasn't buried there. Then my source said, "Oh, I'm sorry, she died."

When I finally gave up, very reluctantly, I shed a few tears and sat at my computer tapping on the keys feeling depressed. I had come so far and looked so hard it was difficult to let go. After a bit I started feeling better and then while pondering what to do next, the words came to me, "What if she's not dead and what if she didn't live in Payson?"

I felt and astounding shock that sent curiosity through my system. Huh? But the family member, who knows her, said she was dead. My curiosity got the best of me and overcame my intellectual dismissal of further effort and started tap, tap, tapping on my keys. Soon I had Ancestry.com on my screen and said, "If she doesn't live in Payson, where does she live?"

"Hanksville," said spirit (or the Universe or whatever you call you intuition)

Outlaws fit in my world nicely, at least Utah's outlaws, some of my favorite Utah Cousins. We are all outside society norms to begin with. That's my heritage and I LOVE every bit of my heritage.

The richness of my heritage makes me what I am.

We Must Be in Utah

Ghosts, Outlaws, Polygamists and DNA, we must be in Utah.

Then in the polygamist column is spirituality with dedication and passion. In the early church, my ancestors saw angels, experienced miracles, had astounding and mighty spiritual experiences. It's all about what you believe and what you can get yourself and others to accomplish...Philosophy driven beings, so, now....

What Lead to This Moment?

Sherma P, who lives in H, Utah. Her sister Elva O had the Bill Long Sister's picture and a letter from Viola, Bill Long's daughter which Bill had told her about his family just before his death.

It was this Viola's Letter and the Bill Long Sister's Picture that put Bill Long's true identity ON SOLID GROUND. When Sherma Peyton was 18 her father, Silas LaVerl Morrell, grandson to Luzernia and Silas

Morrell, Step-grandson to Bill Long, was building the dam at Flaming Gorge. That's when they went to visit Josie Bassett (Morris) who showed them the graves of her 5 husbands. Josie proudly claimed, "I didn't shoot one of them!"

Silas LaVerl Morrell, grandson to Luzernia Ann Allred (Morrell, Long) showed Josie the picture of Bill Long. Josie got a big bright smile of recognition on her face and said, "Sure I'll tell you who he is," obviously recognizing an old friend. Then she hesitated. Her face went sour and she denied knowing him in any way. Interview was over.

Again, this journey on Outlaw Trail Adventures is a spiritual journey, a vision quest of sorts coupled with shaman characteristics. So, hold on for more exciting mysteries moved to the SOLVED column

Embarking on the deepest of Sacred Journeys, one of helping another brother or sister to make the transition from the intense sadness and sorrow of living in shadow influence through the transition into making frequency shifts to the Harmonic Convergence with Creative Intelligence. Simply put. Move from shadow into the light.

What the Universe has guided me to do and what I have come to know as Free Flight Ceremony was honed by the process of fulfilling a commitment to a Ghost. This is my Sacred PATH. Any other path had to fail me because it wasn't my personal connection to the Creative Intelligence that created me and lets me play here. This one on one tutoring is so remarkable that wherever it takes me, I go. Anything less is less valuable and honestly, boring compared to streaming consciousness on the Fabric of the Universe. Now that's fun.

It began many, many moons ago with my heart's desire to experience a fullness of spirit. This spiritual connection fueled by my desires brought to me a powerful unfolding of streaming life experiences which was profound. Life changing, regenerating, spontaneously healing, and self correcting, a true spiritual evolutionary process unfolding before my consciousness taught me more than I had any idea even existed.

That's how we are designed. AND so it was with the creative intelligence which created us and lets us play here. Learning to Live in Harmony with our Intelligent Natures is a process I call Free Flight Ceremony on the Fabric of the Universe. This is the experience I was seeking when I first felt the call to go to a full peyote ceremony with a Shaman, Don. Andreas from Sonoma, Mexico. It started oh so long ago, yet oh so recently.

I had been adventuring into the intuitive realms with a very specific intention: accessing spiritual realms and bring a manifestation into the physical realms...reality as we know it.

In a movie called "17 Miracles" the most desperate and profound of the Mormon Treks across this great continent is captured and embodied in such a manner as to being us to tears with compassion and appreciation for our roots and all it took to get us to Utah.

Word came that the Willies and Martin Handcart Companies were in deep snow and in deep trouble, a rescue was organized. The rescuing parties: Ephraim Hanks first to find them, then Reddick Allred with his wagon and supplies brought them back to the valley. Reddick was first cousin to my third great grandfather, Andrew Jackson Allred who was one of the first people to settle in Wayne County.

Everyone was connected and everyone had to work together to survive and thrive. Jack Allred built a saw mill at Jack's Point on the Fremont River as it flows past the large hill between Loa and Fremont. He built the first trading post in Wayne County.

Regardless of your opinion about religion in general and Mormons is particular, what my people accomplished was often bordering on super human.

If the weather and nature weren't after you, the cattlemen were. If the cattlemen weren't after you, the Indians were. If the Indians weren't after you the US government was sending Johnston's army after you in 1857. And if that wasn't enough, the railroad and bankers were more favorable to the big business and money makers.

Add to "Federalies" coming after your fathers and grandfathers, an eventually your mothers and grandmothers for co-habitation. If they were convicted, they were put in deplorable and horrific conditions in Sugar House Prison across from the old Irving School that has been transformed into a condominium complex.

By the time we are finished with this grand story you will see clearly that I stand on solid ground having spent 10 years working with the latest scientific discoveries in DNA, working thousands of hours on Ancestry.com and with surname projects including Long, Smith, McCarty, Parker and others.

Clear and accurate feedback was my guiding map as I made my way through an amazing array of folk lore, facts, guesses, flat out deceptions and lies and theories that would tie them all together to make the most accurate and viable story about William Henry Long alias The Sundance Kid and the rest of the Wild

Bunch, including Butch Cassidy.

Welcome to my world. Outlaws fit in my world just nicely, at least Utah's outlaws. They are some of my favorite Utah Cousins. We are all outside society norms to begin with. That's my heritage and I LOVE every bit of my heritage. The richness of my heritage makes me what I am.

Ghosts, Outlaws, Polygamists and DNA, **we must be in Utah!**

Then in the polygamist column is spirituality with dedication and passion. In the early church, my ancestors saw angels, experienced miracles, had astounding and mighty spiritual experiences. These have called to me all of my life with a spiritual kinship which crosses all lines. It's a bit hard to explain until you've been there.

But the fascination and passion with which my ancestors lived their lives motivated me to seek and experience things beyond the normal realms of life experience. My passion runs along the lines of Rational Mystic. My standard is high and includes clear and accurate feedback as often as possible to ensure accurate data. Mixed with a lot of hard core traditional research and you get the best of all worlds…an Outlaw Trail Adventure.

While reading Joseph Smith's vision of whom and what we were in our preexistence sparked in me visions of my own. Soon I was remembering and re-experiencing being and intelligence in the preexistence. So super awesome, that I'm still impacted and grateful in so many ways. This part of my awakening taught me so much about myself and about what is available for me to experience in spiritual realms if I am willing to pay the price and prepare to receive and expand into these gifts of understanding.

It's all about what you believe and what you can get yourself and others to accomplish. Philosophy driven beings, so, now....back to the facts as known.

Pedigree Chart William Henry Long

This is the first pedigree chart. We have many, many more Long Family lines. Start here. I would like to give my deepest appreciation for all who contributed to this genealogy and history. The untold number of man hours it took to get this far for me alone has been over 1,000 hours and that was just in the first year on the Longabaugh genealogy. Now we're in year 10...yea, do the math. Now multiply that for every person who, like my beloved grandmother, my father's mother, Luzernia Jackson (Nickle, Baker), who spent much of her adult life at the genealogy library in downtown Salt Lake City, Utah.

I know, I was 5 years old and we would catch the bus every day and go downtown to the library. Her arthritis hands couldn't carry the books, so she would take me with her to carry the books, it was great fun. I remember learning how to read from trying to read the names on the books. I love you grandmother. Thanks for introducing me to the finest ghosts in the eternities...my ancestors.

How could I be afraid of people who loved me? They are my ancestors and it is with the greatest respect I call the Ghosts. Spirits is a more socially correct name, but we are on the Outlaw Trail and this is an adventure of a lifetime so we're all good with calling them Ghosts...especially them.

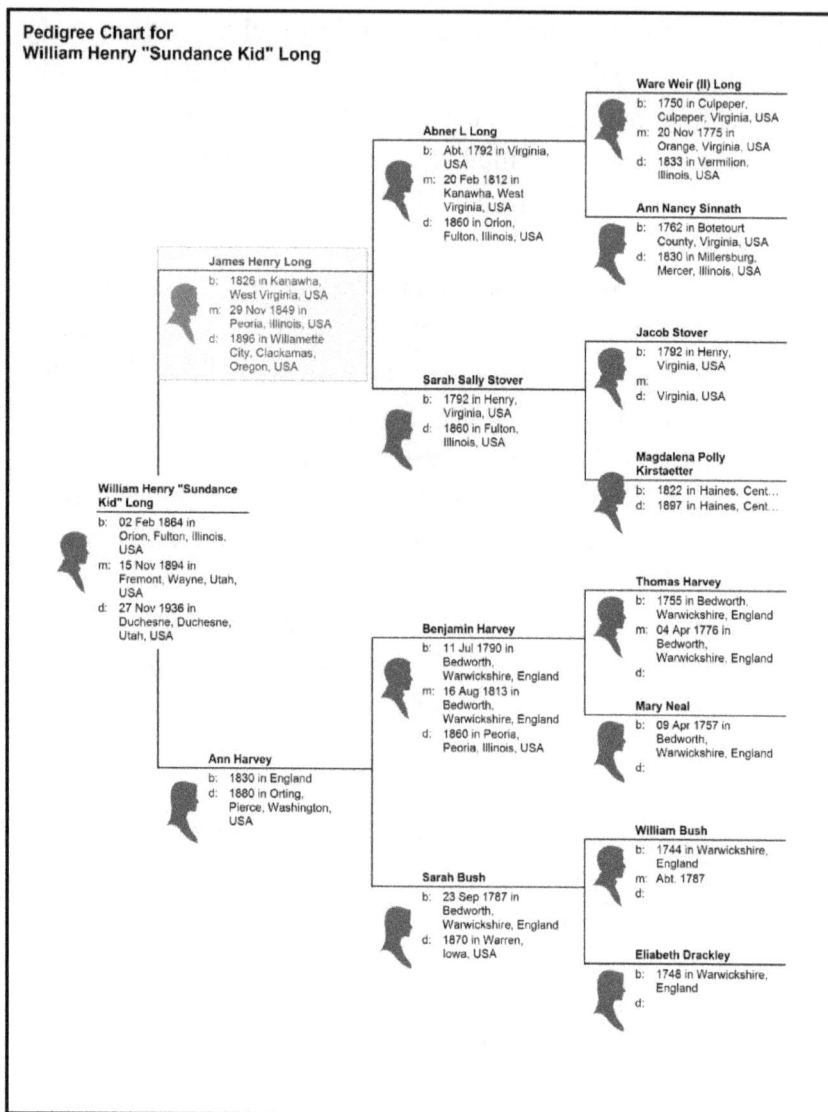

Pedigree Chart for
William Henry "Sundance Kid" Long

William Henry "Sundance Kid" Long
b: 02 Feb 1864 in Orion, Fulton, Illinois, USA
m: 15 Nov 1894 in Fremont, Wayne, Utah, USA
d: 27 Nov 1936 in Duchesne, Duchesne, Utah, USA

James Henry Long
b: 1826 in Kanawha, West Virginia, USA
m: 29 Nov 1849 in Peoria, Illinois, USA
d: 1896 in Willamette City, Clackamas, Oregon, USA

Ann Harvey
b: 1830 in England
d: 1880 in Orting, Pierce, Washington, USA

Abner L Long
b: Abt. 1792 in Virginia, USA
m: 20 Feb 1812 in Kanawha, West Virginia, USA
d: 1860 in Orion, Fulton, Illinois, USA

Sarah Sally Stover
b: 1792 in Henry, Virginia, USA
d: 1860 in Fulton, Illinois, USA

Benjamin Harvey
b: 11 Jul 1790 in Bedworth, Warwickshire, England
m: 16 Aug 1813 in Bedworth, Warwickshire, England
d: 1860 in Peoria, Peoria, Illinois, USA

Sarah Bush
b: 23 Sep 1787 in Bedworth, Warwickshire, England
d: 1870 in Warren, Iowa, USA

Ware Weir (II) Long
b: 1750 in Culpeper, Culpeper, Virginia, USA
m: 20 Nov 1775 in Orange, Virginia, USA
d: 1833 in Vermilion, Illinois, USA

Ann Nancy Sinnath
b: 1762 in Botetourt County, Virginia, USA
d: 1830 in Millersburg, Mercer, Illinois, USA

Jacob Stover
b: 1792 in Henry, Virginia, USA
m:
d: Virginia, USA

Magdalena Polly Kirstaetter
b: 1822 in Haines, Cent...
d: 1897 in Haines, Cent...

Thomas Harvey
b: 1755 in Bedworth, Warwickshire, England
m: 04 Apr 1776 in Bedworth, Warwickshire, England
d:

Mary Neal
b: 09 Apr 1757 in Bedworth, Warwickshire, England
d:

William Bush
b: 1744 in Warwickshire, England
m: Abt. 1787
d:

Eliabeth Drackley
b: 1748 in Warwickshire, England
d:

BILL LONG IS REALLY BILL LONG

The Sundance Kid Alias Bill Long who is Bill LONG
William Henry Long's DNA Comparison
By Bambie L. Reed and D Ross Nickle

5/23/2012 by Bambie L. Reed

THE PROOF IS IN THE COW PIES (DNA)

Genetic match: EXACT MATCH
Genealogy match: EXACT MATCH
Family Names: EXACT MATCH

And the GREAT LONG FAMILY DISCOVERY of 12 Mar 2014 revealed a family secret that has been buried alive for over 120 years: A LIVE Descendent of James and Ann Long has been found in British Columbia, Canada. Vancouver to be exact. A granddaughter in fact, of Bill's sister, Mary Mahalia Long who married James Harvey Brammer. The unlikely chance of finding a granddaughter is astounding in and of itself, however, her life story played out true and accurate. 40 year generations did in two generations what our family with 20 year generations did in four.

Lorna is in fact granddaughter to Mary Mahalia Long, sister to Bill Long. She has her grandmother's death certificate and on that death certificate in 1914, her name is Mary Mahalia Long, just like the sister's name in Viola's Letter. AND the birth date is exactly the same as Mary Mahalia Long AND the birth place, Orion, Fulton, Illinois USA is exactly the same. Her family ended up in British Columbia, Canada have moved up there from Washington State. How much PROOF do you need.

The DIRECT EVIDENCE presented here moves this subject from possible through probably to definitely. The William Henry Long that married Luzernia Ann Allred Morrell in 1894 is in fact William Henry Long, son of James Henry Long and Ann Harvey Long. He was born on the second of February in 1864 in

49

Orion, Fulton County, Illinois.

Time to celebrate...Bill, let's go find a Ghost Dance.

      She, Mary's granddaughter, also has Autosomal DNA which we can compare, for another level of verification. The question is at this point, "Just home much proof do you need?" Some day we might find a copy of the Sister's Picture in the descendents of Bill Long, however, we did the name, birth date, birth place and will have the Autosomal DNA to round up the final pieces. We have more than enough now that the sheer weight of evidences is sufficient to call this part of the case closed. Next.
      And Lorna is absolutely fascinating and delightful with a grand story of true life adventures that got her here, which we will tell soon enough. Meanwhile, here is the old boring science of it all for those who want to walk the DNA trail. Remarkable and educational. What we have accomplished here is astounding. It took 5 generations, research, seeking and discovering, and finally science to give us the final pieces we needed. Enjoy.
Here is are the raw data facts which were fundamental to our proving that Bill Long is in fact Bill Long.

R1b1b2a1a Ware Long Haplogroup, this is the Ware Long who is a direct ancestor of both William Henry Long and William Oscar Long, the two Y DNA sequences which provided the break through to the true identity of William Henry Long.

      William Henry Long, William Oscar Long and Claude Hudson Long are 3 different descending lines of Ware Long II from Culpepper, VA 1720-1803. These are a 15/15 exact match for each of them. SMG Foundation did the testing for William Oscar Long and Claude Hudson Long while William Henry Long's testing was done in the US military

DNA testing lab with Bill Long's bones which were dug up in Duschesne Cemetery, tested and reinterred in 2011.

Result 1 and 3 are both connected to William Oscar Long. Result 2 is a direct descendent of the same Ware Long II as William Oscar Long and William Henry Long.

Within 10 generations there is over 50% probability they are related. This is substantial on it's own merit but not conclusive YET. Bill Long's daughter Viola Long wrote a letter that Ross Nickle found in possession of Sherma Payton, a descendent of Bill Long and Luzernia. In this letter she recorded what her father had told her about his family, his parent's names and his siblings names.

We found a family which matches exactly every family name which are direct descendents from the same Ware Long that has YDNA tests at Sorenson Genetics. The comparison is and exact match, the family names from Viola's letter is an exact match to the genealogy of the YDNA exact matches.

This is CONCLUSIVE PROOF THAT BILL LONG IS BILL LONG, son of James Henry Long and Ann Harvey Long. The exhaustive search is over. There is no more question. William Henry Long is William Henry Long. The proof is in the cow pies. Y DNA testing in conclusive when matched to genealogy and Viola Long's letter. WE REPEAT: Verification includes Viola's (daughter of Bill Long) letter in which she records her father, Bill Long, telling who his parents and siblings are. This is an exact match to the family of James Henry Long, wife Ann Harvey Long, and children exactly as listed in Viola's Letter.

Bill Long is not a Longabaugh. The same Y DNA tests show Bill Long is clearly a Long by Y DNA exact match with other Long surname males. We have 3 Longabaugh Y DNA sets, Gordon Leinbach, David Longabaugh, and Marvin Longabaugh. None of them match each other which was a surprise.

However, they are much more similar to each other tan to Bill Long. I suggest we finish this comparison just for the record. M Amazing Grace claimed in her book she had R Longabaugh's Y DNA, which she in fact did. However, he refused to let her use it once I told him how she was using it. Did I say that she claimed no one had "thought" about getting Longabaugh DNA, she's right, I didn't think about it I DID get Longabaugh DNA! Let's match 'em up and see just how this DNA Shoot Out unfolds!

Hands on your holsters…BANG! I won, Bill Long is not a Longabaugh, not even close. Not even the same Haplo group so this is not a consideration even.

COMPARING WILLIAM HENRY LONG TO THE HARRY LONGABAUGH FAMILY Y DNA FOR 3 MALE FAMILY MEMBERS OF 3 DIFFERENT HEINRICH LEINBACH MALE DESCENDENT LINES

Bill Long is so **not related** Marvin Longabaugh with a genetic distance of 15 in 10 markers, according to my calculations.

Bill Long is so **not related** d to David Longenbaugh with a genetic distance of 16 in 10 markers.

Bill Long is so **not related** to Gordon Leinbach with a genetic distance of 24 in 15 markers.

It is not likely that Bill Long is a Longabaugh by the above comparisons. There is one more comparison available which is R Longenbaugh. We no longer have a reason to continue the Longabaugh comparisons and do not need access to what Marilyn claims in her book. The Y DNA sequences for comparison…this is Marilyn Grace's Y comparison to Bill Long which she claims in her book is a match and proves Bill Long is a Josiah Longabaugh direct relative. There is no way Bill Long is a Longabaugh. ZIP. Notta. Not even close. Not even in the same Haplo group. If you want to believe this nonsense, have at it. I choose to believe the actual scientific data coupled with the genealogy and the Viola Letter. PROOF, real proof.

COMPARING THE 3 LONGABAUGH Y DNA TO EACH OTHER

Marvin Longabaugh is clearly a no match with David Longenbaugh or Gordon Leinbach. There are only 3 markers which match in 12. This is a no match. Marvin Longabaugh has a much closer Y DNA comparison to the Bond Family. This is for them to continue their search. Comparing David Logenbaugh and Gordon Leinbach has a much closer lineup.

CONCLUSION: NOT A MATCH.

Josiah L, Jonas Isaac L, Conrad L 1870, **NO** MATCH TO BILL
LONG
Heinrich Leinback 2755 COMMON ANCESTOR with R
LOGENBACH and Harry A Longabaugh **NO** MATCH TO BILL
LONG
Balsam L, Jacob L, David L, George, Walter Clarence L, Harry L
L, R Longenbaugh **NO** MATCH TO BILL LONG
Bill Long is not a Longabaugh.

This is the Long and Longabaugh of it:

*William Henry Long **is a Long** not a Longabaugh*

It is with a great deal of gratitude for the Longabaugh
Family and their participation in the discovery process. Now, these
conclusion do not yet address who the Sundance Kid is, when, why
and how. I am stating here that yes, Harry Longabaugh was the
original Sundance Kid that was arrested for stealing the horse in
Wyoming and put in jail by Marshall Ryan.

**BUTCH CASSIDY IS RELATED TO HARRY
LONGABAUGH IN BEAVER, UTAH**

However, while wandering through The Outlaw Trail
Adventures Data Base of Genealogy I found that Harry
Longabaugh has relatives in St. George, Utah. One Sarah Smith
whose father was John X Smith. John X Smith emigrated from
England after he joined the Mormon Church and was disowned
from the family which was well off at the time. This one of these
relatives married a relative of Butch Cassidy, Ebenezer Gillies.

Her mother was a Patterson who is from a MEGA POLYGAMIST FAMILY, we'll go into all of those connections when you have evolved through this entanglement into enlightenment and start to see the whole picture of what was really going on out her is the Wild West.

Anyway, Harry Longabaugh, the original Sundance Kid escaped and because Sheriff Ryan didn't get paid if he didn't have a prisoner, he was hard pressed to have one in his jail. Enter William Henry Long. Now the first description of Harry Longabaugh b the Marshall fit Harry Longabaugh exactly. but the second description of The Sundance Kid when he was captured two weeks later was not at all the same.

This description fits William Henry Long. Bill Long may well have been in the Deadwood, South Dakota, going by the name of MODOC Bill. There was a Bill Long alias MODOC BILL in the Deadwood area. William Henry Long's father, James Long, married the widow Lucy Ann Baldwin and moved the Willamette Valley after 1880 when Bill's Mother, Ann Harvey, died on the Asotin Plateau, Washington State where they had immigrated to from Orion, Fulton, Illinois along the Oregon Trail. WHEW! What a mouth full.

Why is this important? Because the MODOC Indian tribe was a phenomenal tribe who were extremely resilient. Led by Captain Jack, their chief, they were the last Indian tribe to avoid being captured and annihilated with their remnants being put on reservations in the entire United States. It took a small fortune for the Indian fighters to finally run them into the lava fields of their final stand in Oregon and annihilate all but 400 who were moved to a reservation.

This was the final chapter in how well white man integrated into this great land. Anyway, Bill using MODOC BILL would be a natural consequence of all of this. He would have been 15 or 16 when his mother, Ann Harvey, died and then would have moved with his father James, his new wife Lucy Ann and their combined families. Their children were many. The MODOC BILL story is still in the discovery stages. So, let's get back to how MODOC BILL, or Bill Long, came to be known as the Sundance Kid. Let me go on record right here with what I believe to be the rest of the Sundance Kid story.

Much of my story about the Sundance Kid is generally accepted as accurate. Some of my story about the Sundance Kid is my best information put forth in the most accurate representation of what I have discovered and how I believe it to have been. Much of my discovery process is centered around a 60,000 name genealogy data base I call the Outlaw Trail Adventures Data Base.

It is not complete by any means, however it reveals over and over and over how people, places, dates all accumulate together to give a presentation about events. Much of the data is good solid here they are, this is who lives in the area, and this is what is likely correct about their relationships.

ON SOLID GROUND WITH BILL LONG

The most educated estimation available. This is what I used to complete the Bill Long story to this point. The information about Bill Long and his DNA and his genealogy are . Way beyond estimations, they have been scientifically proven and now we have found his Grand Niece, granddaughter of his sister Mary Mahalia Long and her husband James Harvey Brammer out of Washington State and Canada.

Great Story by the way and it's all true and verifiable and verified. We have Bill's other sister from the sister's picture, Sarah Sabina Long who lived and died in Steilacoom, Pierce, Washington right on the Puget Sound.

This is how I stored my data, found these people, discovered great stories and people and put the puzzles together over and over and over again. Looking at the astounding data revealing amazing connections in time and space in the form of people's lives and shared events. So, here we are, having traversed this steep mountain range of treacherous and confusing often conflicting data, focused, clear and moving forward powerfully. Now is the time to share this grand adventures I have had the incredible opportunity to live on Outlaw Trail Adventures. Welcome to the Fabric of the Universe where we are all connected in the most intriguing and interesting of ways. Just when we were sure we were alone in the world...

For those members of the family who have been in the influence of M Amazing Grace, look carefully at this work and know that it is thorough. The one thing I learned in these 10 years is that the closer you get to what really is, the more data you find at a certain point. Arduous process as you well know. I am sharing with you what I have learned and hope you enjoy the process of discovery for yourselves.

DATA AS IT RELATES TO THE LONGABAUGH FAMILY LINES
Here is the Longabaugh DNA Y LINE UP:
Harry Longabaugh: Heinrich Leinback, Conrad, Jonus I, Josiah and Harry Longabaugh

David Longabaugh: Heinrich Leinback, Conrad, George, George W, James, Earl Elias L, and D Longabaugh. (12 markers Y DNA test)

Gordon Longabaugh: Heinrich Leinback, Conrad, Samuel, John, Allen Frederick, Willard, and G Longabaugh. (37 markers Y DNA test)

We have two sons of Conrad, George and Samuel and their descendant lines, these are the most likely to line up with Harry Longabaugh.

Marvin Longabaugh of Las Vegas: Heinrick Leinback, Balsam, Jacob, Samuel, George, William H, Jackson M L, William T L (12 markers Y DNA test)

R Longenbaugh of CO: Heinrick Leinback, Balsam, Jacob, David, George, Walter, Harry, R Longenbaugh (12 markers Y DNA test can only tell you who they are not related, not enough information to tell you who they are related to. A 15 marker match is good but more data is needed for proof.)

These Longabaugh lines are from Conrad's brother Balsam and his son Jacob with their descendant lines. These two are less likely to be a match due to genetic distance and mutations which occur. However, you never know until you do the science. Remember: The Proof is in the Cow Pies.

Marvin's is not a match, however, his line has the most genetic distance and is least likely to match. Gordon and David have similar markers to each other, not an exact match but with a genetic distance of 3 in 12 markers, it is worth pursuing a 37 marker for David and then see how they compare.

With the known genealogy connection and the same surname, it is likely they will prove out. The best opportunity for establishing a likely Y DNA for Josiah Longabaugh, is to have another Y Longabaugh DNA sequence as close to Josiah as possible. Preferably several more, however, one more will likely give us enough information to reveal the likely Josiah Longabaugh Y sequence as closely as possible, none of this is useful to us any longer.

We are done with the Longabaugh of it.

Science has given this gift of understanding DNA and who is who which should be fully utilized to resolve a 5 generation mystery. In the DNA Long Longabaugh Shoot Out was on the 4th of July 2012 in Hole In the Wall, Wyoming I revealed in detail the proof that Bill Long is a Long. With the help of 4 remarkable Morrell kids we showed the world unequivocally that Bill Long is Bill Long, son of James Henry Long.

William Henry Long is my second great grandfather (step) who came into my family when my great great grandmother Luzernia Ann Allred Morrell was about to lose everything. Bill Long saved the family farm, finished raising her 6 children, added two more to our family, and was father-in-law to Jeremiah Jackson who shoed horses for Butch, Sundance and the Wild Bunch. It is my sincere desire to make sure all claims about him are backed up with as much proof, actual scientific and research as available to us.

If we can show more proof that Bill Long was the Sundance Kid, we will be the first in line to celebrate, though Uncle Jerry has presented a great case that Bill Long is the Sundance Kid, at. However, there is sufficient data showing that Bill Long is Bill Long along with the DNA Y sequence proof and research data to back up the proof. See Outlaw Trail Adventures on Facebook for more details.

The Long Surname DNA Project

http://www.longwebs.org/longdna//Participants.htm

Once Ross and I Dug up Bill Long's Bones and Sorenson Genetics was gracious enough to do testing on his bones with their brand new testing process, we came up with 7 markers. (This test was a $10,000 gift) 7 markers is enough to come up with a no match in comparison with others, but difficult to clearly say he's a match. If you get a 7/7 match, then you can say he may well be, however, more markers are needed. At that time, there was no way to get any more markers.

Bill Long had only daughters and we had no identity for Bill Long. The following 3 people showed some promise on the Long Surname Project pages. However, at that time we compared Bill Long's 7 markers with the Longabaugh Y DNA and Tim Kuberschmidt at Sorenson Genomics said they were a NO MATCH. This is all we came for at that time and we were still pursuing Bill Long's true identity. 7 markers wasn't enough to be a substantial match with confidence.

DIGGIN UP BILL LONG'S BONES, THE REST OF THE STORY

Jerry and Judy Nickle took their turn at the whole process, dug up Bill Long again and had Tim K do forensics on Bill Long's bones along with more DNA testing. They went it to the army DNA lab and got the 16 Y DNA markers for Bill Long we are using now. This is much more substantial than the original 7 markers.

At this time I posted the William Henry Long information including the Bill Long Sisters Picture and the Viola Letter on my web page. Ross and I also posted the actual Y DNA sequence. A fellow researcher brought in the James Henry Long family census which helped tie in with the real Bill Long family.

Jerry and Judy Nickle found the William Oscar Long Y DNA match. Ross had found this early on and did not pursue it due to the 7 marker limits and we had gotten the results that Bill Long wasn't a Longabaugh. Time marches on and things continue to unfold and change…

We embraced the Y DNA results that show Bill Long is William Henry Long descendant in the Ware Long family. So if we put the piece together we find:

(7) Robert Jackson Long #10* is a descendant of Nicholas Long of Caroline Co. VA (and later Campbell Co., Kentucky).

R J Long is in the SG data base and is one of the 3 of the 15/15 markers match for Bill Long.

My second great grandfather is William Henry Long. I have just linked his genealogy to

(29) Robert Long #18* is a Ware Long descendant. His great grandfather was David Long, who settled in Linn County, KS ca. 1857, with his brothers, Madison and Myron Long, sons of Abner Long of Gallia Ohio.

William Oscar Long from SG database is a 15/15 match and it looks like the Y DNA test from his great grandson, though this is private information which we lined up with the Long Surname projects family lines and they are a genetic match and a genealogy match. This along with the Viola Letter naming William Henry Long's siblings…exactly along with his father and mother exactly is substantial and proof that William Henry Long is William Henry

Long.

RESOURCES:

http://www.familytreedna.com/pdf-docs/Interpreting-Genetic-Genealogy-Results_web_optimized.pdf

This is KEY to understand the genetic distance information…a must read for those who want to understand how we came to believe Bill Long is Bill Long, not a Longabaugh, he is in fact Bill Long with Y DNA matching the Long Family surname.

THE PROOF IS IN THE COW PIES (DNA)

Genetic match: EXACT MATCH
Genealogy match: EXACT MATCH
Family Names: EXACT MATCH

AND we have an exciting breakthrough which finalizes our proof out of Vancouver, British Columbia, Canada.

MARY MAHALIA LONG (BRAMMER) SISTER TO BILL LONG ALIAS SUNDANCE

DRUM ROLL: Mary Mahalia Long, the youngest sister of Bill Long's, contacted me on Facebook. Her unbelievable and amazing story started with finding a genealogy message I had left in the Brammer Family on Genealogy.com looking for Mary Mahalia Long who married James Brammer. Are you ready for this?
Are you sure? This is it. This is the missing link that is sure proof that Bill Long is the William Henry Long that we have proven him to be. Just for those who are emotionally attached to The Sister's Picture that hung on the wall at Grandpa and Grandma Long's two story house in Duschesne, yet the same one that the kids would sing the S&S, M&M sisters song about Grandpa Bill's sisters, S&S for Sarah Sabrina and M&M for Mary Mahalia…you remember, the picture that everyone thought was lost in the fire

with mysteriously showed in the closet of a Morrell Family granddaughter. That was a great gift...

So we all fell in love with Bill Long's Sisters all over again and the search that has been going on for 10 years plus 3 generations starting with Florence Viola Long, Bill's daughter and her mammoth efforts to find her father's family. It all finally came together three days ago on March 12 at 11:14 pm while I was checking Facebook for the days entertainment...Lorna, granddaughter to Mary Mahalia Long was contacting me asking me if I wanted to talk about her grandparents, Mary Mahalia Long and Jimmy Brammer.

My mind melted down and incredulous as I felt, I came to long enough (almost fainted with sheer excitement) to say yes. We have so much we have been sharing, discovering, enjoying about the Long Family and the connections we have.

Lorna is from Vancouver, British Columbia, Canada and her understanding of the country, the people, the French language that was and is prevalent. And another piece of insight to the language Bill Long came back speaking, French, Mary Mahalia's youngest son, Lowell, (who is also Lorna's father) when he was 4 years old he remembers his mother speaking....FRENCH! Interesting. Pieces and bits, each one precious.

Long time family lore has it that Bill Long went away for a long time, years. When he returned, he was speaking French. Another powerful verification putting yet another clue solidly in place for our William Henry Long mysterious puzzle.

This along with the Viola Letter naming William Henry Long's siblings...exactly along with his father and mother exactly is substantial and proof that William Henry Long is William Henry Long, son of James and Ann Long.

Thanks Grandpa Bill, it is an honor to have walked with you for these many years and these many miles with this whole passel of people connected to you. I trust that this is what you desired when you asked me to help you heal yourself, your family and move into the light. If not, you know where to find me. Love, Bambie your loving second great granddaughter. There's always another grand adventure when Bill Long is around.

Relationship: William Henry "Sundance Kid" Long to Robert DNA MATCH WHLJackson Long

Robert DNA MATCH WHLJackson Long is the 5th cousin 3x removed of William Henry "Sundance Kid" Long

4th great grandparent

Jeremiah Long	Eleanore Francis
b: 1644	b: 1648
London, England	Essex Co, England
d: 1687	d: 1687
Rappahannock, Virginia, USA	Rappahannock Co, Virginia, USA

3rd great grandfather / 4th great uncle

Richard Long	Gabriel Long
b: 1729	b: 1663
Spotsylvania, Spotsylvania, Virginia, USA	Essex, Virginia, USA
d: Aug 1762	d: 1750
Caroline, Virginia, USA	Caroline Co, Virginia, USA

2nd great grandfather / 1st cousin 4x removed

John Long	NICHOLAS LONG
b: 1700	b: Abt. 1684
Culpeper, Culpeper, Virginia, USA	Essex County, Virginia, USA
d:	d: 31 Jan 1750
	Orange, Orange, Virginia, USA

Great grandfather / 2nd cousin 3x removed

Ware Long	Jeremiah Long
b: 1720	b: 1728
Culpeper, Culpeper, Virginia, USA	Caroline County, Virginia, USA
d: 1803	d: 1756
Culpeper, Culpeper, Virginia, USA	

Paternal grandfather / 3rd cousin 2x removed

Abner L Long	Nicholas Long
b: Abt. 1792	b: 15 May 1754
Virginia, USA	Caroline County, Virginia, USA
d: 1860	d: 13 Oct 1846
Orion, Fulton, Illinois, USA	Newport, Campbell, Kentucky, USA

Father / 4th cousin 1x removed

James Henry Long	Richard Pickett Long
b: 1826	b: 11 Jul 1784
Kanawha, West Virginia, USA	Caroline, Virginia, USA
d: 1896	d: 22 Nov 1853
Willamette City, Clackamas, Oregon, USA	Independence, Jackson, Missouri, USA

Robert DNA MATCH WHLJackson Long is the 5th cousin 3x removed of William Henry "Sundance Kid" Long

Self

William Henry "Sundance Kid" Long
b: 02 Feb 1864
Orion, Fulton, Illinois, USA
d: 27 Nov 1936
Duchesne, Duchesne, Utah, USA

5th cousin

Robert Nicholas Long
b: 27 Oct 1823
Blue, Jackson, Missouri, USA
d: 29 Mar 1885
Jackson Co, Missouri, USA

5th cousin 1x removed

Robert N Long Jr.
b: 11 Jul 1866
Missouri, USA
d: 05 May 1931
Independence, Jackson Co, Missouri, USA

5th cousin 2x removed

Claude Hudson Long
b: 11 May 1889
Missouri, USA
d: 07 Sep 1938
Independence, Jackson, Missouri, USA

5th cousin 3x removed

Robert DNA MATCH WHLJackson Lon
b: 23 Feb 1920
Texas, Missouri, USA
d: 21 Mar 2005
Independence, Jackson, Missouri, USA

Just in case you were getting bored with Bill Long's DNA:

And the next challenge: What did Charley Anderson, Hiatt Morrell and Bill Long all have in common?

The surprise may shock you...and no one is talking about it. In fact, get near it and people start diving for cover. I knew the story is out there and will find its way home to me in its own due time.

They all died within a month of each other. Charley Anderson had cancer, Hiatt died from blood poisoning and Bill Long killed himself. Now I don't know about you, but this isn't just right. The three of them used to hang out together, Bill Long's death may have been murder and blood poisoning from appendicitis could be a cover for other things. I'm just saying it's very peculiar, especially when there are family rumors saying Matt Warner went on a hunting expedition at the same time death was occurring.

Research project anyone?

They say a family member in Hannah, Utah knows more... They say the funeral home in Roosevelt knows more but isn't saying. Let's get after these projects and finish up Bill Long's Life History right. With the Grand Finale he deserves and we desire.

NOW, JUST IN CASE ALL THAT SCIENTIFIC PROOF ISN'T ENOUGH, HERE'S THE MITO SIDE OF THINGS: Mito is the marker we get from our mothers.

The Proof is in the Cow Pies

A Story About Bill Long's DNA

By Bambie L. Reed

With Excerpts from D. Ross Nickle

THIS IS A COMPARISON OF the mitochondrial DNA of William Henry Long and Harry Longabaugh using the DNA of Dr. Ogden Frazolle Edwards with permission from his descendents.

In the 1990's, Ann Meadows, Dan Buck, Clyde Snow and others traveled to Bolivia and exhumed the bones of two banditos from the states. In this process, they used a live Longabough mitochondrial descendent to compare DNA to. That sequence belonged to Dr. O. Frazolle Edwards, now deceased. They also exhumed the bones of Harvey, Harry's brother in Massachusetts. They determined that it was likely that Mr. Edwards was related to Harvey, although, Mr. Edwards was nonrelated to the banditos (in South America). We were able to obtain exclusive rights from Mr. Edward's descendents to obtain that sequence. We then compared Mr. Edwards sequence to William Henry Long and found that they were not related."

From an article "Digging Up Bill Long's Bones" written by D. Ross Nickle in 2010 and published on:
www.outlawtrailadventures.com and
http://www.facebook.com/events/272441119518946/ in 2012.

Harvey Longabaugh, brother to Harry Longabaugh the traditional Sundance Kid shares the same mitochondrial DNA. The "proof in this cow pie" shows that Dr. O. Frazolle Edwards descendent of Mary Tuston born 1793 died 23 Feb 1837, daughter of Thomas Tuston and Mary Smith.

Tim K of Sorensen Genetics verified what our conclusions were:

That Bill Long's Mito DID NOT MATCH Dr. O. Frazolle Edwards Mito.

NOT A MATCH.

With this established, we now have the question of the hypothesis being researched by Marilyn Grace and her team which is printed in their book, "Finding ""The Sundance Kid"" Solving The "Wild Bunch" Mystery by Marilyn Grace and John McCullough, Ph.D.

In her book in the "GUILTY" As Charged! section, Marilyn writes, "*Emma Longabaugh was conceived when Josiah Longabaugh was in the Civil War. Was Josiah her father? The family bible only has the year she was born, 1863. Didn't the Longabaugh's know when their child was born? Harry Longabaugh only has about 1867.

Why didn't the family have the day and month Harry was born. *Were both Emma and Harry adopted into the family* and they didn't know their birthdays?"

She also wrote on that same page, "*We may have the Longabaugh family living in Port Providence in 1867*, and Harry A Longabaugh is born in Mont Clare. "Sundance" was 3 years old when he appeared on the 1870 census record living with the Longabaugh's. *Bill Long's DNA genealogy belongs to the Jacob Family* that settled in the state of Pennsylvania. Some questions still need answers, but we believe we have the bulk of our research completed." All I can say is show me.

I bolded the significant statements for clarity. "*Were both Emma and Harry adopted into the family*" can be solved easily with one comparison. We know that Harvey Longabaugh's mitochondrial DNA MATCHES his second cousin 2x's removed Dr. O. Frazelle Edwards. We have Dr. O. Frazelle's Mito for comparison.

Harvey Longabaugh's maternal lineage is not in question in

Marilyn's scenario.

Marilyn Grace and her team have the Mito from Carl E Schuch. Carl is a 4th cousin 1x removed of Dr. O. Frazelle Edwards and both theoretically if everyone is who they say they are on the genealogy charts should match and would establish the mitochondrial markers for Annie Place Longabaugh, mother to Harry Longabaugh.

If the Mito comparison of Dr. O. Frazelle Edwards matches the Mito of Carl E Schuch, then William Henry Long's MITO is not a match to Carl E Schuch as sit was not a match to his cousins. You can then extrapolate that Bill Long is not Harry Longabaugh. This does not mean he is not The Sundance Kid, however. My uncle, Jerry Nickle is bringing his book and documentary out soon. This will present his research showing Bill Long is Bill Long son of James Long and that he is The Sundance Kid...not Harry Longabaugh.

If the Mito comparison of Dr. O. Frazelle Edwards does not match the Mito of Carle E Schuch his 4th cousin 1x removed, then someone along his Mito line is not genetically who they appear to be. If they do not match then Marilyn's theory may prove out if you can find the Jacob family she is alluding to.

We don't need Marilyn Amazing Grace and her camp to bring their Mito to the table any more. We have the proof and will continue to reveal and guide the discovery process for all who wish to venture forth.

The relationship charts below show the relationships. Thomas Tustin and Mary Smith had many children both in England and then in American. There were 3 sisters born here, Hannah, Mary and Rachael. We now have mitochondrial from a descendent from each of these three sisters. Harvey Longabaugh from Rachael who's is a close match to the of Dr. Ogden Frazelle Edwards, a descendent of Mary Tustin. And the latest from the third sister Hannah is Carl E. Schuch. If the third one matches, it establishes a probable mitochondrial for the Tustin line including Ann Place Longabaugh.

I predict that all three mitochondrial results are a match establishing a probable Mito for Ann. I also predict that Harry Longabaugh is in fact his mother's son..son of Ann Place Longabaugh.

Again, with DNA results all bets are off until the final drum roll and I'm hearing a final drum roll here…finally. Or, just another drum roll and we're off for more testing…which is what usually happens.

Again, we don't need any more comparisons for proving Bill Long is Bill Long. The final results are here for your research. Bill Long is William Henry Long, son of James Henry Long and Ann Harvey Long, son of Abner Long Descendent of Ware Long.

THE PROOF IS IN THE COW PIES (DNA)

Genetic match: EXACT MATCH
Genealogy match: EXACT MATCH
Family Names: EXACT MATCH

WILIIAM HENRY LONG IS A LONG

CHAPTER 6

The Sundance Kid's Long Lost Sister is Found

Bill Long and Jose Bassett

Sherma Peyton, granddaughter to Grandpa Sundance, had the original picture of Bill Long, The Bill Long Sisters Picture and Viola's Letter. It was this letter, written by Bill's daughter Florence Viola Long, and this picture that put Bill Long's true identity ON SOLID GROUND. When Bill Long was about 21 years old, someone brought a picture of his sisters to him and he reconnected to his family in Asotin, Washington.

When Sherma Peyton was 18, her father was working building the dam at Flaming Gorge. That's when they went to visit Josie Basset. That's when Ann Basset, after looking at a picture of Bill Long, said, "If you knew who he was, you would want to kill yourself."

The only interpretation that I make here is that she knew him, she knew his identity would have impact and perhaps not in a good way so why did Josie Basset know Bill Long and have such a reaction to his picture?

According to Sherma Peyton, granddaughter of Hiatt Morrell, daughter of Silas LaVerl Morrell, Josie's first reaction to seeing a picture of Bill Long was a big warm friendly smile and saying sure, then a hesitation, then a frown and shaking her head, "No, I don't know this man."

As all of this sinks in, I'm going back to The Sundance Kid alias William Henry Long whose life is progressing nicely and whose story comes back into play so you can keep up with the significant happenings on our Outlaw Trail Adventure.

When Two Kindred Spirits Meet

The spirit of her son was adamant that she research their genealogy and family lines. He was very insistent upon her doing this, his name was David and he was her son who had died. As Lorna, my Canadian Cousin, sat there in the morning sun in Phoenix, Arizona where she spends the winter telling me of how she came to seek me out I was spellbound.

She did as her son had requested and while researching the Brammer Family Genealogy, she came across a message on genealogy.com which I had left there many, many moons ago hoping, desperately seeking as Bill Long sibling descendant, preferably a Mary Mahalia Long or Sarah Sabina Long live descendant.

As I returned to the scene of the original post on the Brammer Family Forum, there were the tracks I had walked on 6/25/13. Leaving bread crumbs so to speak for someone to come find me who knew Bill Long's family and wanted to make the connection.

I have left thousands of messages over the last 10 years and only once in a blue moon does someone come forward to answer me. This was one in a million. This was the jackpot and Lorna Brammer French found my message while seeking her grandmother Long's family.

Here's my post:

http://genforum.genealogy.com/brammer/messages/266.html

James Harvey Brammer, 7 May 1864

Posted by: Bambie Reed (ID   **Date:** June 25, 2013 at
*****6737)   11:25:38

| 266 | Go |
of 266

Looking for the family line of James Harvey Brammer, b 7 May 1864 who married Mary Mahalia Long b. 1869 in Orion Fulton, Illinois.

Looking for their descendents. Claud (Cloude, a French name), William, Keith and Lowell and their descendents.

Would love to find the live descendents and make some exciting connections.
Thanks,
Bambie

My mind drifted back to when I met:

Bill Long, The Only Grandfather We Knew

He's as much of a grandfather to me as my own grandfathers. For 10 years I have followed him through thick and thin, come hell or high water and have torn down barriers, lived through family feuds, uncovered deep dark secrets long buried alive and pretty much changed history.

It has been a wild ride and we will prevail...I met him the first time at a haunted house in Herriman, Utah when I described him to 6 other people and a digital video camera caught his essence on film along with some orbs which had been with us in our meditations that night.

And so it started. A week later I found out he was my second great grandfather, William Henry Long. It has been a wild ride...Ghost Riders of the Wild Bunch. They came forward desiring to move into the light.

And each in turn I helped them do whatever they needed to finish their business through genealogy and family histories and connecting live descendents. Much of this work is still in process and about to launch to the next level of awareness where everyone gets to meet Bill Long's Ghost. That's what he said and so far, everything Bill told me has come to pass.

So, here we are, on the verge of the break through which changes everything. With deep gratitude I go forth having come here to heal myself along with Bill Long. May the Highest Outcome for all unfold as we go forward. And so it is...I love you Grandfather Bill. It is an honor to ride with you.
Lorna's son DAVID:

The Spirit of Bill Long's Great Grand Nephew

This is the important part: Lorna, my Canadian Cousin, was telling me she had started down this genealogy path, finding her ancestors when her son died and she felt compelled to search for their ancestry. She spoke of how often David came by in his spirit to talk to her, encourage her and sometimes strongly motivate her to get this job done. David's influence is what lead her to look on genealogy.com on the Brammer Family message board where she found my message:

http://genforum.genealogy.com/brammer/messages/266.html (shown above)

Bill Long's grand niece, Lorna Brammer French, granddaughter of Mary Mahalia Long who is Bill Long's sister was on my Facebook account hunting me down. I opened my Facebook and was watching a conversation going on between my good friend, Christine Fisher Thiessen, whom I met on the Long Family DNA Project.

Imagine looking for someone who had lived 100 years ago for 10 years and you open your Facebook page and you find they are taking to a good friend of your on your account! Yes, I'm saying it was thrilling!

Conversation on Facebook Revealed the Sister of Sundance

This is the conversation on Facebook that changed everything.

The Discovery of Bill Long's Grand Niece Lorna

Lorna, from British Columbia, is the grand niece of William Henry Long. This is sure and absolutely accurate proof of Bill Long's true identity...William Henry Long, son of James Henry Long and Ann Harvey. However you may choke on that information, it goes down smoothly and easily once you do the "due diligence", apply science and stay sane through the insanity of it all.

FACE BOOK LIVE:

Bambie L. Reed: 2 hours ago The Civil War has some history not generally known, while looking up Bill William Henry Long, The Sundance Kid, stories, specifically the cowboy camps he went to when he was six years old to get away from his father who raged at him for riding the horse that was pastured after the horse brought his brother Abner's young body home, having been killed by Indians...anyway, Bill lived in the cowboy camps for quite a while. I wanted to know more. I was in hot pursuit of a live descendent to help prove Bill Long is Bill Long by YDNA, I got this message from a here-to-for unknown granddaughter of Mary Mahalia Long Brammer, sister to Bill Long.

HOUSTON, WE HAVE A LIVE DESCENDANT IN THE LONG FAMILY!
FIREWORKS, WELCOMING MAT
WELCOME TO OUR PART OF THE FAMILY, LORNA AND DAVID

The conversation that changed history and brought together the families of William Henry Long and his sister Mary Mahaila Long Brammer.

Lorna French: "Is this a relation of James Harvey Brammer, b 7 May 1864 who married Mary Mahalia Long b. 1869 in Orion Fulton, Illinois?"

Christine Fisher Thiessen (A great friend of mine and Long Family DNA Project coordinator) Yes, this is.

Lorna French "Do you know the name of Mary Mahalia Long's parents? She was in the right place at the right place at the right time."

Lorna French "No, but she is my grandmother"

Christine Fisher Thiessen said, "James Long and Ann Harvey-Long had a daughter named Mary that was born in 1869 according to my records. She would have been a sister of William Henry Long. This James Long was the son of Abner Long and Sally Stover-Long. Abner died in Orion, Fulton, Illinois, in 1860."

I WAS EXTHATIC! A LIVE DESCENDANT WAS TALKING TO MY LONG FAMILY DNA Project Coordinator LIVE, AND I WAS WATCHING IT! So, I jumped in.

Bambie L. Reed "Yes, Bill Long's sister's name was Mary Mahalia Long, she's the youngest of the siblings of James Long and Ann Harvey. This is a great conversation, thanks by the way. YES, YES, YES, this is the James Harvey Brammer who married this Mary Mahalia Long."

• **Bambie L. Reed**
https://www.facebook.com/442557549091077/photos/pb.4425575
49091077.-
2207520000.1394649766./661412730538890/?type=3&theater

This link will take you to the Bill Long sister's picture on Facebook.

Family Lore speaks of hearing the children singing the family song of Bill Long's sisters Sara Salina and Mary Mahalia the S&S, M&M sisters.

Bambie L. Reed, "Lorna, here is our picture of Mary Mahalia Long and Sarah Saline Long. William Henry Long's two sisters."

Bambie L. Reed that's Sarah Salina or Sarah Sabina Long, it's hard to read the hand writing...Sarah, may have married an Abraham Hamilton, not as clear on that one and am still looking for more info on the whole family of siblings and their descendents.

http://www.outlawtrailadventures.com/.../Sisters_Photo.html

Where the story started...

www.outlawtrailadventures.com

Starting in the Fall of 2004 we had several interviews with a direct descendant ... The above post is about finding the Bill Long Sisters Pictures which was a great gift and precious to us a few seconds ago. Now, the connection is established and the information verified. We really do have a live descendant of James and Ann Long, sister to Bill Long, one of the two sisters in Bill Long's Sister's picture. None other than Mary Mahalia Long. Bill Long's sister. The final proof that will turn the hearts of the family to the truth about Bill Long and his lineage.

Thank you Lorna for finding my message I left oh so long ago on genealogy.com and looking me up. You are such a great and exciting gift. WOW is all I can say...thank you Bill and everyone else along the way on this great Outlaw Trail Adventure which is really an extension of my Optimal Life PATH Spiritual Adventures Club. My spiritual path lead me to meet this ghost which lead me to the Outlaw Trail which lead me to Bill Long and this lead me to Lorna French who's son's spirit guided her to do the genealogy which lead her to me.

And so it goes in the grandest scheme of adventures...life. How fun is this? The very best LIVING LIFE has to offer.

The Grandest of Ghost Stories Comes Full Circle

So we have come full circle with the Grandest of Ghost Stories. From meeting the Ghost of the Sundance Kid 10 years ago to being guided by another ghost, his grand nephew, 10 years later, we heal a family whose identity was torn apart 150 years ago. Now that's a ghost story to tell your kids!

And to complete the circle that started when I met the Ghost of William Henry Long alias The Sundance Kid, today I found out that Orrin Porter Rockwell helped settle Bluffdale, Utah. That's the same place where I met Bill Long's ghost in the old haunted round rock house 10 years ago. I've asked the question of Bill, "What here?" It's took 10 years for this answer to come full circle. Here is the part that Orrin Porter Rockwell played in settling the area where I met Bill Long's Ghost in 1994.

According to Wikipedia, Bluffdale, Utah, named for its geography of bluffs and dales, was first settled in 1848–1849. On July 29, 1858, Orrin Porter Rockwell paid five- hundred dollars to Evan M. Green for sixteen acres of land near to the Crystal Hot Lakes (adjacent to the present Utah State Prison).

This land included a hotel with dining facilities, stable, brewery, and pony express station. As the community expanded, the Bluffdale area became part of South Jordan, then Riverton. In 1883 the Bluffdale School Precinct was formed from parts of Herriman, South Jordan and Draper. On August 1, 1886, the Bluffdale Ward of The Church of Jesus Christ of Latter-day Saints was organized with Lewis H. Mousley as Bishop. For a short time the town was called Mousley.

There are seven irrigation canals that originate at the Jordan Narrows in the Bluffdale area and serve the Salt Lake Valley. One of the earliest was the Utah and Salt Lake Canal started in 1862. Some of the early buildings included an adobe church, built in 1887–1888, a tithing house, and a three-room schoolhouse constructed in 1893.

Though Orrin Porter Rockwell died when Bill Long was about 20 years old or so, Porter's role in shooting the great uncle of Etta is noteworthy. This brings my connections full circle and I realize that I had to come this way, all the way back to the old rock house where I met the Ghost of The Sundance Kid.

This place and its history connected all the stories I've been gathering for 10 years to help Bill Long heal and most into the light. There are many who wish to make the jump to light speed. These powerful indicators of connecting evidences make such a strong grid of evidences that their profound meanings bring it home to our hearts and minds.

The rest of the history of Utah is richly ingrained in family lore, local historical evidences and genealogical connections. If enough people relate to my story and buy enough of my books, I can go back and piece it all together so you can share the solid ground upon which my stories are built. This is as far as I can go so far, but there's so much more that I will tell about as things evolve and information comes together.

One of my greatest heart's desires was to have a story come out of Bill Long's research which would blow us out of the water when it came to spiritual realms interacting with physical realms. This does it!

This is the exciting part of all of this, as clear and accurate evidence of energy realms interacting directly with physical realms. Now, each of us will interpret this how we may, but I'm telling you this is a very exciting day for me, as a Professional Remote Viewer, a Hypnotist, and a Suburban Shaman, this is where all my worlds come together. I have been able to capture in real time some very exciting and powerful experiences of a profound proportion. So let's continue of this grandest of spiritual journeys.

As you walk between the worlds with me, you must do what Crockett the current day "Long Rider Cowboy" who took me into Robbers Roost said when I asked him how to ride this large brown mare down the thousand foot sand cliff on a tiny trail, "Just don't fall off! Oh, and don't hold on the horn either or you'll fall off over her head!

"Yousa", that was a moment to hang on to, I decided it was a great day to die and what better way than on a horse going down a thousand foot sand hill in Robbers Roost! Life doesn't get any more exciting than that.
So, if you have the courage to stay on your horse, let's ride on down into the Roost.

Come Hell or High Water

The Ghost of the Sundance Kid, William Henry Long, Speaks
AND MY PROMISE TO THE GHOST OF THE SUNDANCE KID

Current Date: 4/16/14

Timeline Date: August 2002

Location: Herriman, Salt Lake, Utah

Come Hell or High Water I've proceeded to do exactly what I promised the Ghost of The Sundance Kid I would do. I'm a psychic medium, remote viewer, hypnotist with a holistic health focus. The last thing I was interested in was an outlaw. But once I met Bill Long's Ghost, I made a promise to help him heal and help his family heal and move into the light.

And that's exactly what I've waded through hell and high water for, riding off a thousand foot sand cliff and sleeping on a rock in the desert for, driving all night to get to Washington to get DNA from the McCarty Family for, and on and on and on. None of the discomfort mattered at all, only the great journey.

The road blocks, the thieves that stole my stories that I have gleaned from so many kind family members and hours, days, weeks, months and years of research, the disinformation spread by some so they could profit from that which they stole. The lack of being acknowledged for the significant contributions I shared openly.

Having my best works "borrowed" became a common place experience, yet I knew I needed to contribute still for it would bring about the right sequence of people, places, events and ideas to prepare for the real story line of Bill Long's life to come together as he wanted it to be. And so we proceeded. I learned quickly to not judge the outcomes for what seemed like a bad outcome most often led us in the right direction for a better outcome.

And so the WILD BUNCH HEALING CEREMONY that began the moment I met the Ghost of the Sundance Kid has guided my life through a much more interesting and profound series of life changing and profoundly enhancing, soul expanding and just plain thrilling and giggly fun adventures.

My greatest heart's desire has always been from the time I was 5 years old, to enjoy my spiritual adventures which have come so spontaneously to me and then share them with others to let them receive the great opportunity to experience how much more we are than we think that we are.

I specifically asked the universe for a spiritual adventure so remarkable that people would listen to me, get that this spiritual adventure I am on is real and interactive in physical reality and find it all to irresistible to not dabble with. Just play a little bit here, a little bit there and soon you will know for yourself whether it's worth your time. For me, there was no turning back. It has been just too much fun to live any other way.

In the year 2001 while working with a group of my close friends, Annie and the kids, honing our Remote Viewing skills every Thursday night around Annie's kitchen table or in her breathtakingly beautiful garden with handing blooms and night blooming flowers. Great times, growing times, grand adventures of the Fabric of the Universe.

Since I'm confessing, I guess now is the time to tell you the rest of my story so you will know of which I speak. This will set the background for you to understand why the Ghost of the Sundance Kid came to me that night in Herriman, Utah while we were exploring the "haunted rock come house".

My life is rich and full in every. The greatest desires of my heart have always come to me, though there were struggles in learning about my relationship with the Fabric of the Universe. The people I needed when I needed them always showed up, right on time, even though often I wasn't patient enough to be joyful until the perfect time. I learned by trial and error.

Full of determination and the willingness and ability to endure are gifts of mine I have always been grateful for and believed whole heartedly in my Patriarchal Blessing given to me when I was 16 by a Stake Patriarch in the Mormon Church. From the moment he uttered those words I knew they were right, true and correct for me and that they would guide me my entire life, not matter what else happened, or what else I might believe. I knew deeply these words were true and the depth of the depth of their meaning still astounds me.

Awe and gratitude fill my soul. For without them, I wouldn't have known that I could go through all I went through and come back safe, strong and empowered. It was never a question when it was time to take a journey through soul work, I knew I could do it and make it back intact with gifts for others when I came.

Full speed ahead, now I've let others tell their tales and I really appreciate the incredible ride we have been on. Outlaw Trail Adventures is not for the faint of heart and weak of mind. The San Raphael Swell is unforgiving to the foolish and the selfish. This is a time for setting the record straight and so it is with Bill Long's guidance and a lot of work, we have come this far and have been richly reward if remarkable life experiences. Thank you, Bill.

On one of the many occasions I had given up in frustration and impatience, the universe came on by one more time and awakened my senses, opened my mind and gave me what I need to continue. This is what guidance I did receive that got me to write this book.

LIVING GUIDANCE FROM THE FABRIC OF THE UNIVERSE AND THE CREATIVE INTELLIGENCE WHICH LOVES ME AND LETS ME PLACE HERE ON THE OUTLAW TRAIL IS AS FOLLOWS:

People love Butch Cassidy and the Outlaw Trail. Write Bill Long's story straight up, powerfully, fully, FULL ON CONSCIOUSNESS with what is and whatever is less than this has to disintegrate. Focus on wholeness and the highest within you to ascend to.

My Sacred Path is to share what I've learned with those who come after me. This is not what I expected nor is it something I would have chosen for myself before entering upon this sacred path. Yet, now I'm here, I am thrilled at the remarkable journey I've had the privilege to take. I am so grateful for every person I've encountered upon the way. So listen up, we have work to do.

My highest path is so much more fun than I ever thought it could be. What could be more fun than riding a horse over a thousand foot sand hill cliff down a narrow path into Robbers Roost sitting on the same 10 foot wall that The Sundance Kid, Butch Cassidy and Etta used for protection in the winter of 1896 after the Castle Gate robbery?

I'm going to get a few things straight right here. Charley Gibbons, owner of a general store in the Utah Settlement of Hanksville during the 1890s, said Butch always paid his debts and "always paid cash." Kelly, in his book, 'The Outlaw Trail' wrote, "All old-timers interviewed for this biography, including the officers who hunted him, were unanimous in saying, 'Butch Cassidy was one of the finest men I ever knew.'" Butch was Robin Hood with a Colt .45, and enough sources attest to his decency streak that it's probably true.

Real life in the Territory of Deseret was much different than anything you or I have had to live through. For 50 years the polygamists out here in the west were fighting for the survival or themselves and their families. They were "outside the law" according to the United States Government who sent Johnston's army in 1857 to squelch the "Mormon Rebellion".

Now this is where the real story gets extremely interesting. Did you know the real Etta, the "first Etta" in Butch's life was a Utah girl? Oh, yes, and I'm going to provide enough evidence that you too will come to understand Utah, polygamy, the wild west and outlaws, especially The Wild Bunch like never before.

A Freedom Loving People

These are my people, Utah is my home. My ancestors left their homelands during the 1600's when John Lathrop fled tyranny after spending 7 months in the Tower of London for printing books on FREEDOM! In the 1700's my ancestors came, escaping from tyranny, in the 1800's my ancestors were again seeking a better life out of the burden of tyranny and the rest of them came to America. But life here wasn't exactly a bed of roses.

And then the Civil War with all its bloody and abusive impacts from those who sought to make others do their bidding as slaves and or other tyrannical policies and laws. All of these connections, all of these ancestors, all of these courageous and fascinating people made the Wild Bunch and all the intrigue and fascinating adventures in living life through the challenges of the Old West and settling the frontier here in the desert of Utah.

In Utah, we are all cousins. If your grandfathers and grandmothers were polygamists, you are a cousin of some sort with everyone else. Just do the genealogy and the math...three wives with 15 kids and then in one generation they marry into 45 other families...voila cousins and cousins and cousins. It's great.

When I grew up here in Salt Lake City, Utah, my neighborhood was remarkable for kids to prosper and grow in. When our chores were done, we would all gather for the daily adventures of youth in Utah. When we needed feeding whoever's mom was round would feed us. When we needed spanking, whoever's mom was around would spank us.

There was a great comfort and strength to have a village so strong and compatible to support the greatest growth for its youth. That was the good side of it. There was a shadow here and there as there always is in life. But we'll keep moving through it all and back to the ghost stories.

This impact of growing up was from my polygamist ancestors and all of my cousins and their cousins. We take care of our own and don't tell others anything...for all these generations, except every now and then when it's expedient. It's now expedient and Bill Long wants his story told.

And, all this being equal on spiritual adventures, I get to live this most glorious spiritual adventure and it's so worthy of sharing that everyone wants to at least look this way and see what Butch Cassidy has to do with a healing ceremony.

Now back to our story line. It is well to remember as we journey through 150 years of time that judgments about others are not even useful. The point here is that one moment you were a decent person and the next you were outside the law.

The cattlemen were powerful and dominant and changed the laws to suit themselves. The wealth of the time was cattle. The cattle wars in Wyoming alone were bloody, full of murder and dishonorable acts from all walks of society, everyone trying to use the resources of the west to promote their own well-being, whatever that took.

As you read these stories, these experiences and more especially these spiritual adventures disguised as a great life adventure chasing outlaws, just be ready for a soul expansion. You will see things in a new light.

Whether or not you are yet awake enough to hear my voice and find your place among those who are awakening and being the enlightened version of the empowered creators we all are will impact not only you but the entire collective. Especially now, everyone counts. So heads up, let the journey begin.

The intuitive guidance from the Universe continued, "None

of this is a mistake and you will be guided, as usual. Your mission, should you accept it, is beyond anything you've ever imagined before.

Because you have chosen to have compassion for and empathy with your ancestors here in the west from the age of 5, you have been prepared to serve them as you wished to do with all your heart, might, mind and strength.

As you watched that western and saw the evil preacher preaching guilt, shame, fire and brimstone while he took the money from the people to save them from evil you could clearly see at the ripe old age of 5 that this was not right. And you were very passionate about being like the other preacher who was traveling from home to home, farm to farm blessing, helping, and working as need be.

Really helping the people he showed true love and compassion for all. Powerfully my little heart and mind said, "Count me in, I want to serve the people of the west like the good preacher." And so it is, your wishes are granted.
In the interim time you have lived a rich life and have been guided through so many experiences in places of both good and evil and you have been preserved safely.

As you have been promised in your blessings, you are one who can walk these paths safely where others would have fallen prey to the shadows that befell them. Not that you weren't tired, honed, strengthened and challenged so you could be ready when it was time to do what you came here to do. Show the way for others who need a light while you take on shadow and shift it back into its harmless and formless nature, whatever the optimal outcome is for all.

WELCOME TO THE FABRIC OF THE UNIVERSE

And so it is for now..." Love," the Creative Intelligence, says, "Welcome to the Fabric of the Universe." With all its creative forces and flowing energies creating great lives for us and with us this is going to be a great time. Let's play.

Awakening, spirituality, the path to WHOLENESS, ASCENSION this is what I'm all about. This was my PATH, my Portal Access to Hyperspace as the Remote Viewing world calls access to intuitive or spiritual realms of information. This was the beginning of the Outlaw Trail Adventures that have transformed and changed everything, making my life a whole lot more fun than sitting of a cloud somewhere singing lofty songs.

So here we are, raw and wriggling, the adventure begins. Remember, I warned you that listening to what I have to say will change you. A soul expansion is on its way and you will get to see the old west and Butch Cassidy, The Sundance Kid, Etta, (especially Etta), Tom, Matt, Bub and the rest of the Wild Bunch from a whole new perspective. Good luck with that, this is gonna' get fun.

Whatever you do, don't fall off y'er horse.

CHAPTER 7

Ghost Riders: More Than One Sundance Kid

The Ghost of the Sundance Kid
Alias William Henry Long

In a nutshell this is what you've learned so far:

This is a very true story which began an Outlaw Trail Adventure the day I met the Ghost of the Sundance Kid. Come Hell or High Water I would help him come into the light where he could feel the powerful loving feelings of having overcome the powerful forces for darkness and the unbelievable depth of sadness which had haunted his heart and mind for 115 years.

And so it began, my incredible journey to help my second grandfather, William Henry Long, The Sundance Kid who served 18 months in jail for stealing the horse that Harry Longabaugh actually stole. He was totally exonerated for that one, not so innocent on the rest of his story. Oh, he also used the alias The Sundance Kid upon occasion. See my Uncle Jerry Nickle's book, "Bringing the Sundance Kid Home."

I agree with much of what my Uncle Jerry wrote though I have strong evidence that there is much more to the story of The Sundance Kid. William Henry Long did use the alias of The Sundance Kid as did at least 4 of them total, William Henry Long, Harry Longabaugh, Hyrum Beebe and Frank Smith (another known alias of The Sundance Kid).

The brilliance is this tactic was a powerful and effective way of keeping everyone safe. Outlaws, their often polygamist families, friends and the towns they lived in.

It is known that Bill Long had a good buddy named Matt Warner, known outlaw, member of the Wild Bunch. Matt shared a bank account with Bill Long until the stock market crash of 1929 which depleted the money for everyone and left the Long's with barely enough to get by on.

Bill was no longer his young strong tough body had long since aged like everyone's does and arthritis had set in. When Sorenson's Forensics analyzed his bones, they said he had arthritis, a serious case of it and that he was likely in a great deal of pain from it. They also said that his bone density which tell you how strong he would have been in life was the most dense they had ever tested. Bill Long was tough physically, the toughest.

William Henry Long, Beloved Grandfather

After the stock market crashed it was tough to keep going with little money, health deteriorating, his wife had been bed ridden for two years from diabetes, and the infamous Bill Long, the toughest of the tough, was getting too old to keep up with it all. They stayed with their daughter Viola Ehler in Midvale, Utah for a winter and then the depression made even that too much. Bill and the family had a major discussion which became a fight...in the morning Bill Long was dead on the wood pile, dead at age 72.

Having fought one hell of a fight he died having taken care

of his beloved wife for 42 years, helped her raise 6 children and their two children. Bill Long was the only grandfather the Morrell children knew. Silas had died before any of the grand children were born.

William Henry Long, beloved husband, dedicated father saved the family farm in Wayne County, he made it so Luzernia could keep the land she and Silas Morrell had homesteaded and built up, he raised the kids and grand kids, tended the farm and ranches and lived a most remarkable life. He was also a folk hero.

Grandpa Sundance saved the cattle the year the snow storms were so bad most cattlemen lost a lot of their herds. He risked his life and limbs through the cold and blizzards to get the herd to a lower pasture where they could find food and water and be out of the deathly cold mountains.

He taught uncle Perry how to shoot in a way that would save his life. "Here," Grandpa Bill said, "put your pointing finger along the barrel like this. Point your finger and pull the trigger with your next finger. Otherwise, you don't have time to aim then shoot or you are already dead."

Life skills that are useful in the west. And Bill Long was the best of the best. Now there is some very exciting news from the Outlaw Trail News Desk: They are reporting that Bill Long and Luzernia lived next door to Etta, the first Etta that Butch feel in love with in Milford, Utah in 1894-1896.

At least her father George was their neighbor. AND it just so happens that Hiatt Morrell, son to Luzernia and Silas Morrell, stepson to Bill Long married a gal named Ruby. Ruby Lazenby had a father like most of us do and his name was Walter Lazenby.

Walter had moved his first wife, Mary Cook Lazenby, out to Fish Creek, Utah in Wayne County where they were raising their 5 children. Mary died in child birth and left Walter with 5 babies to raise. He soon married Mary Nadine Ames and they had 10 more wonderful and amazing children. Why do we care about Ruby and her sister Nadine?

Well, well, well...now that's a strategically significant question to answer. Strategic to what, pray tell, what can be so important about Fish Creek, Wayne County, Utah in 1896 no less?

DRUM ROLL.... (come on someone give us a drum roll...[drum roll] there we are, thanks)...

Etta, the female outlaw that ran with Butch Cassidy and The Sundance Kid? Remember her, you know, think "Raindrops Keep Falling On My Head" and the bicycle ride in the movie "Butch Cassidy and The Sundance Kid".

Yes, the young, the stunningly beautiful Etta. About 5'3" tall, stunningly beautiful, came from a very musical family who had a family band called The Rocking Chair Band and her uncle and aunt were in the Payson music scene which had phenomenal musicianship, born in Payson, Utah in 1877. This makes Julia Etta Ames the exact right age for the descriptions of Etta, was in the same place at the same time as Butch Cassidy in an era where Milford, Utah and Beaver Bottoms had big dances and an extremely popular dance hall, and she and Butch would have both been at "A Wedding in Panguitch", Utah, 22 Mar 1893. Here's how the story goes.

Once upon a wild western time…

There Once Was A Wedding In Panguitch

Panguitch, Utah that is. Robert LeRoy Parker would have been at that wedding, most likely. And Julietta Ames most certainly would have been at that wedding because the bride was her sister, Rosina Ames.

Now these girls are half sisters to Mary Nadine Ames who married Walter Lazenby who had a daughter named Ruby who married Hiatt Morrell, the stepson of The Sundance Kid. Bill Long and "Zernie", as she was called, lived for a time next door to George Monteville Ames, father to both Mary Nadine Ames

(Lazenby) and Julietta Ames. The same Juliette who was at "A Wedding In Panguitch."

Now, that's a lot of cow pies to wade through, so keep your boots on and don't squat on your spurs. Just remember in our story, THE PROOF IS IN THE COW PIES! Cow Pies you say? Yes, DNA, the straight proof no holds barred. So, get back on your horse and learn to keep up. Oh, you might want to wash your jeans you didn't listen to me when I said *don't squat with your spurs on*! Next time, you may want to listen carefully and hear what I have to say.

Then you can feel free to get very excited about what really happened here in Utah. Oh, by the way, we are all cousins here in Utah. It takes a lot of powerful and remarkable people dedicated to building a better life for themselves and their families, forever families, performing in powerful, positive, progressive and profound ways. That's a lot and that's what it took and more.

The Ghost of the Sundance Kid, Harry Longabaugh

My Uncle, Jerry Nickle, wrote a book called, "Bringing Sundance Home." He goes through a great deal of effort to show that the original Sundance Kit was indeed Harry Longabaugh. You can check his book out for a detailed explanation of his findings.

I agree with most of what he has to say up to the point where he has William Henry Long as the only other Sundance Kid. I believe he did indeed go by the alias The Sundance Kid upon occasion, especially in Wyoming where he spend 18 months in jail and then was totally exonerated.

Now realizing that Hollywood is just that, Hollywood, and they are in the profession of making movies and making lots of money making movies. The content whether accurate or not is secondary to the story, unless they are doing a documentary and then it's up for proving whatever they wish to prove to the best of their abilities.

That's as good an explanation as I have found out there, so let's go with it until further notice. But, that's not where the story ends. Survival in the late 1800's had become treacherous. Many of the Wild Bunch were dead, in prison, or hiding out in South America or the like.

Hiding your true identity became a matter of life and death not only for you but for your family as well. Now, on top of that, there was this other side to the Utah Territory and the polygamists who lived here.

The "Federalies" as grandma used to call them were agents sent by the US Federal Government to find, harass and arrest polygamists. It was a question of becoming a state for the Utah Territory and that was a big deal, but wouldn't happen while polygamy was being practiced.

And so things heated up here in the Old West, especially the territory of Utah or Deseret.

There are those who claim that Hyrum Beebe was the Sundance Kid. He was raised in Circleville, Utah and lived in Rockville, Utah with his Native American Wife. The Terry Family tell the stories of how he was known as The Sundance Kid. And he certainly acted the part by being a recluse with violent tendencies when someone crossed his path.

His family was out of Circleville, Utah. So he certainly would have had a lot of opportunity to know Butch Cassidy. His family was also filled with Polygamists. His genealogy connects him strategically to many of the Mega Polygamist Families.

Now that term, MEGA POLYGAMIST FAMILIES, one I coined to give us a better understanding of just how we are talking about, why the genealogy of the Wild Bunch is important and how Ghosts, Outlaws, Polygamists and DNA are all connected. It's a wild and wooly tale and we are just getting started.

By the way, if you have any Utah Pioneer Ancestry, pull out family histories and genealogy charts because you are going to want to see how you are related to Butch Cassidy, The Sundance

Kid, Thomas Jefferson, Jesse James, Cole Younger, Belle Starr, Brigham Young, Joseph Smith, John Lathrop, etc, etc, etc. It's a Wild Bunch and they all played their parts in getting us to where we are today. I'm telling you now, you don't really know who your cousins are, yet, but you will...

So let's shock your delicate senses with the cousins Harry Longabaugh has in Beaver, Utah. You heard it right, Beaver, Utah. Birth place of Robert LeRoy Parker. The Beaver, Utah, that Butch was born into in 1866 on the 13th of April was much different that the peaceful town it is now nestled in the foothills below Panguitch Lake and the most wild and exquisitely beautiful country you've ever laid eyes on. From red rock country to pine forests to Panguitch Lake in all its splendor.

Along with the majestic beauty are the shadow that linger at Meadow Creek, down the mountain from Panguitch Lake. It all started just before the time of The Mountain Meadow Massacre. Proctor Robison and his companion William Young were guarding the cattle from the Fillmore, Utah ranchers.

About the time the Fancher Party came through the area, the springs were poisoned at Meadow Creek. William Young and Proctor Robison became deathly ill when they drank from the springs. William Young told Proctor to get on the only horse they had and ride to Fillmore as fast as possible. Proctor was worse off than William and took off. He made it back to Fillmore, but died by morning. It was a horrible death.

[Proctor Hancock Robison's body has since been exhumed and the forensics are suggesting the perhaps it was anthrax and that the poison was inadvertently spread to the corn creek Indians and Proctor Robison by the Fancher Party cattle getting a drink on Meadow Creek from which they all drank. Fascinating to consider the implications. Be it what it may, it's history now.]

Meanwhile word of William Young's plight send rescuers to find him as he was trying to make his way off the mountain from Meadow Creek. They retrieved him, bought him home to Fillmore and tended to his dying process and within a week he too died from the poison in the spring at Meadow Creek or Panguitch Lake, depending on the version of the story you are reading. I suspect that William Young had more to do with Panguitch Lake and Proctor Robison had to do with Meadow Creek. I will report more as I find it. This was one of the things which lead up to the Mountain Meadow Massacre.

Those who say poisoning the springs did not happen, need to talk to Proctor Robison and William Young. Oh, that's right, they died. As with all stories in life, there are many facets to every story and always things we don't know. It took over 150 years and science to get this piece straight. Doesn't change the outcome, but it does sober us and hopefully keeps us sane when faced with difficult choices in life.

Many, many things happened around the Mountain Meadows Massacre time, some of which are of interest to our story. Proctor Robison was a son of the richest man in Utah at the time, Joseph Robison.

Now, Joseph Robison, gave my great uncle IG Robison several thousand dollars which was a small fortune at the time to help him start his businesses in life. IG Robison married Clara Morrell the third sister in the Silas and Luzernia Morrell family. That's the same Luzernia that married the Sundance Kid. These connections keep coming full circle.

IG Robison was a fine rancher and farmer who named one of his beautiful daughters Etta. He openly told her she was named after Etta, the female outlaw that ran with Butch Cassidy. IG Robison had a ranch on the upper part of Trachyte Canyon. This canyon has spectacular hiking through red rock slot canyons and amazing parts of the desert here in Utah.

There's a rock in the middle of the canyon on your way down to Lake Powell which used to be called mail rock. This route was taken to deliver the mail to the local towns. Now this information really connected back to The Sundance Kid alias William Henry

Long, since IG Robison was his son-in-law.

The Ghost of the Sundance Kid, alias Hyrum Beebe

When Hiram Beebe first arrived back in Southern Utah, he made his presence known by his erratic behavior. On October 17, 1935, he was charged with malicious mischief On June 18, 1938, he was charged with vulgar and abusive language, for which he got six months in jail in November 1938.

Upon completion of his jail sentence, Hiram Beebe rented a house and property just across the old bridge spanning the Virgin River in the little town of Rockville, Utah, close to Zion National Park. Here he lived with his common-law wife Glame, Paul Millet, and Frank O'Banion.

The house was rented from Arthur Terry, and, in 1980, eighty-eight year old Marvin Terry, Arthur's brother, remembered the unlikely little group. He recalled that Beebe was about 5 feet, 9 inches tall, sturdily built, sometimes smooth-shaven, sometimes with a beard. He described Beebe as a "grouchy egotist" who traded at Terry's general market which is now a residence.

Terry recalled that Beebe would sit in front of his house and watch the cars driving along the state road across the river. Terry's father was accustomed to taking a short-cut across Beebe's land on his way to visit one of his sons. One afternoon as Terry passed the house, Beebe began "yelling and cussing" at him, brandishing a gun, and warning him that if he ever caught him there again he would shoot him.

The elder Terry complained to the sheriff who paid a visit to Beebe, warning him not to repeat the threat. Beebe went to prison for shooting a sheriff, and died there. So the legend lives on about his role in playing out the saga of the Sundance Kid.

An Article appeared in the 1989 issue of The "Beebe Connection" Newsletter by the then Editor, Mary Beebe. She wrote, "The City Cemetery was developed in 1848 one year after the Mormon pioneers arrived in the Salt Lake Valley. It is the largest city owned cemetery in the U.S. Included in the 300 acres is the grave of Hiram BEEBE, reputed to be the Sundance Kid of Butch Cassidy and the Wild Bunch fame."

She continues, "In 1986, I visited City Cemetery and saw where Hiram and his wife are laid to rest. The death certificates were obtained from the local Mortuary that had performed the funeral duties for the two.

While talking to the office personnel, at the cemetery, they told me that after Glame collapsed at the prison and was pronounced dead, on her possession they found an enormous amount of money in the hem of her dress. Also, they told me that they had to pour a huge amount of concrete in the base of Hiram's stone to hamper vandalism of the tombstone.

Hiram and Glame are not buried side by side but across a road from one another. Hiram's case caused much controversy but aren't we lucky to have such a celebrity? Much information about his trials is reported in the newspapers and certainly make for interesting reading."

Newspapers which were quoted in the article were: Desert News, Salt Lake Telegram, Thursday, June 2, 1955. LDS Library, Salt Lake City, Utah Desert News and Telegram, Salt Lake City, Utah. Monday, Jan. 5, 1953.

Another entry from Genealogy.com, "He was arrested by the Sanpete County Sheriff and posse in 1945 for shooting down and killing Mount Pleasant City Marshal Lon Larsen. Beebe was convicted and sent to Utah State Prison where he served until his Death. Beebe was known as fanatic and antisocial in the central Utah communities where he lived. Some believe that his true identity was Harry Longabaugh, the famous train and bank robber also known as the Sundance Kid. This identity has never been proven and Longabaugh's family denies the possibility. Beebe was extremely fast and deadly with the pistols he always carried, and sort of looked like an older version of the Sundance Kid..."

Well, they can't all be THE SUNDANCE KID, right?

Uhhhhhhh, yes, they can. It seems in the grand scheme of Butch Cassidy's Wild Bunch World, every scheme in the book and many more were used to stay on top of the "outlaw game". In other word, staying alive and thriving amidst daily threats of survival and attack. So, pull out all stops in your brain, and realize these folks were clever, very clever.

Well, I found a probable genealogy for Hiram Beebe. His father would have died in Circleville, Utah, in 1884. He father's name would be William Albert Beebe. Their relatives are interesting and their location of Circleville, Utah, where Butch Cassidy's family was living tells me we probably have the right one. More Discovery Needed...but, he's not my focus so I give him to you if you are so minded.

The more believable Sundance Kids you have, the more cover you can establish. It's a brilliant strategy. The following relationship chart shows how Hiram Beebe (Joseph Hyrum Beebe) is related through John D. Lee to Butch Cassidy and he grew up in Circleville, Utah.

Relationship: Joseph Hyrum SUNDANCE BEEBE to Robert BUTCH Leroy Parker

Robert BUTCH Leroy Parker is the step grandson of half sister of husband of niece of Joseph Hyrum SUNDANCE BEEBE

Parent

William Albert Beebe Sr	Louisa Newton
b: 09 Jun 1813	b: 11 Aug 1819
Greenville, Greene, New York, USA	Berkshire, Massachusetts, USA
d: 21 Dec 1864	d: 1886
Circleville, Piute, Utah, USA	Aurora, Sevier, Utah, USA

Self / **Brother**

Joseph Hyrum SUNDANCE BEEBE	LeRoy Winslow BEEBE
b: 05 Jul 1850	b: 25 Jan 1840
Pottawattamie, Iowa, USA	Sheridan, Chautauqua, New York, USA
d: 03 Jul 1920	d: 05 Oct 1912
Lethbridge, Alberta, Canada	Clark, Nevada, USA

Niece

Lydia J Beebe
b: 09 Jan 1877
Virgin, Washington, Utah, USA
d: 13 May 1961
St George, Washington, Utah, USA

Husband of niece

Elisha Lee
b: 20 Jul 1862
Kanarraville, Iron, Utah, USA
d: 15 Mar 1937
Sparks, Washoe, Nevada, USA

Father-in-law of niece

John Doyle LEE
b: 06 Sep 1812
Kaskaskia, Randolph, Illinois, USA
d: 23 Mar 1877
Washington, Washington, Utah, USA

Half sister of husband of niece

Louisa Evaline Lee
b: Abt. 1850
d: 04 Sep 1932
Panguitch, Garfield, Utah, USA

Louisa Evaline Lee Born 1850 was the daughter of John Doyle Lee and she married Butch's grandfather, Robert Parker had a son Maximillian Parker from his first of 3 wives. Max Parker married Annie Gillies and they had a son Robert LeRoy Parker...Butch.

The Ghost of the Sundance Kid, alias Frank Smith

Now this is my particular favorite of the Sundance Kids, next to Bill Long, simply by the added benefit of having been married to Etta. The Etta that Butch Cassidy first fell in love with in 1892-1894.

Rumor has it in the Morrell Family that William Henry Long and Frank Smith rode into Fremont, Wayne County, Utah together somewhere between 1891 and 1894.

Another of my Utah Cousins, Steve Taylor, says that his mother who lived in Fremont when Bill Long lived in Fremont while he was married to Luzernia, insists that Bill Long was "one of them, one of those who rode with the outlaws."

Remember that she lived in Butch Cassidy territory near Hanksville, Utah; in the same town as the Zufelt family that Matt Warner's second with belonged to and the same town that The Sundance Kid alias William Henry Long lived in. In fact, she was a Taylor cousin to the Morrell's. William Henry Long was married to Luzernia Ann Allred Morrell in 1894. So, she should know, she's one of the Utah Cousins.

Again, everyone has cousins, but not one has cousins like Utah has cousins!

Ancestry.com is our Bible here on Outlaw Trails Adventures. From the moment we set foot into the Long and Longabaugh of the Sundance Kid's Ghost Story, we began to find connections using genealogy, pedigree charts, family histories and whatever else we could to make these connections. You see, in Utah we are all cousins. Really. Even The Sundance Kid alias Harry Longabaugh. No, he's no Mormon you say. Well, listen up, the gossip is really going to fly about this connection.

This is better than going to Relief Society and finding out all that's happening in Utah. Oh, that's right we are the families of the Relief Society sisters and we get to tell the whole story. It was the dedicated Relief Society Sisters over generations who submitted

98

their genealogy and family histories faithfully and with appreciation and honor, serving their ancestors.

This is a great gift to all of us. So, listen up kids of all ages, you don't want to miss this one. This is the most interesting adventure into genealogy that you'll ever come across. Who knows, you might even find yourself wandering around on these pedigree charts.

Oh, Okay, if you're going to whine about not getting a peek preview about how Harry Longabaugh is one of our Utah Cousins, here you go. See Ghost of the Sundance Kid, alias Harry Longabaugh section and look for the name John X Smith in the last chapter.

Back to the story of Frank Smith. There are 3 strong possibilities of who he is if you ask his YDNA. After searching for 8 years for Frank Smith through trails and tales, YDNA, Autosomal DNA, and everything in-between.

His YDNA is out of The Netherlands and Smith is one on the likely surnames. At least there was a partial answer.

And so the pursuit began. I didn't really want to go here. It's a lot of work and it's not easy work. But then in the middle of the night this Ghost came to me while I was puttering with questions on Ancestry.com. Well, you know by now how I am with ghosts who have a mission they want me to perform for them. And so it is that I came to research Frank Smith.

Welcome to the Cove, Sevier County, Utah

Then, they moved back to, of all places on earth, Joseph, in Sevier County in Utah. In fact that's mighty interesting because Julietta Ames was now living in the Joseph area working at a boarding house in Cove.

The only problem I could see was there wasn't a Cove in Sevier County. So, the journey of discovery began as we search for Cove in the pages of history. Yep, certainly was a Cove, Utah. In fact, Cove was a remarkably fascinating place when young Julietta lived there.

And the timing was amazing, 1896. Now why is that even interesting at all? Follow the clues. Julietta had been living down in Milford, Beaver County, Utah from 1894 through 1896. She had been dating some young men whom her father, George Monteville Ames had found so displeasing that he forbade his young and very beautiful daughter to date.

Now Milford, Utah was in its heyday. It had a large dance hall filled with music, dancing and a great time. Julietta lived in Beaver Bottoms, near Milford at the time. There were cattlemen and miners in abundance.

Another interesting person enters the picture. Robert LeRoy Parker worked for James Ryan and his ranch was very near Milford, Utah, about this same time. How convenient. This makes it probable that they danced at the same dances, knew the same people and ran into each other at least once or twice.

Oh, that's just where our story gets warmed up, there are more connections between Miss Julietta Ames and the man who would become famous known as Butch Cassidy. Outlaw of the Robin hood flavor.

Julietta had another probable meeting with Butch. Her aunt, Sarah Angelina Eames who was married to David Alma Losee lived in Panguitch, Utah, 8 miles from the Parker Family home in Circleville. Now David Alma Losee was quite the musician and played for dances and was involved in community bands.

In 1892 there was "There Was A Wedding in Panguitch". Julia's only full blooded sister, Rosina, got married. She married Milford Bard Farnsworth. Now Milford Bard Farnsworth had a brother, half-brother with the same father and another mother, yes he was a son of polygamists. One of the MEGA POLYGAMIST FAMILIES that play such a dominant in significant role in our story of Etta, Butch, Sundance, Tom and the Wild Bunch.

Why his brother Cyrus and a son named Cyrus Walter

Farnsworth is interesting is because he married Eva Clara
Bentenson, Butch Cassidy's aunt. So THERE WAS A WEDDING
IN PANGUITCH which changed everything. This was the first of
many astounding connections between Butch and Etta and Frank.

Frank Smith rode into Loa, Utah with Bill Long in the early
1890's. Bill Long is my grandfather give or take a couple of
generations. I have proven he is really William Henry Long son of
James Long and Ann Harvey, son of the Ware Long family lines
so well researched by the Long Family Surname Project. (They
have helped our journey tremendously.
They are the group who came up with the William Oscar Long Y
DNA originally and connected the Ware Long pedigree charts
which made it possible to connect Bill Long to his Y DNA exact
match 17/17 William Oscar Long.)

So the initial question was who is this man who rode into town
with Bill Long? Not too much of an attention getter, one of those
put it on the back burner though. Until I was handed this name and
my brother said, "Don't spend too much time on this, it's probably
nothing."

Within 3 hours I had found Julietta Ames grew up to become
Julia Etta Ames who married Frank Smith. Likely that same Frank
Smith who rode into Wayne County with Bill Long. And little
Julietta Ames opted to have her name changed from her birth
certificate to Julia Etta Ames on her headstone. And that's where it
got really exciting.

ETTA...the name itself is full of beauty and intrigue.

I was so thrilled that I jumped in my car and drove the two
hours to Price, Utah. After locating the cemetery, I found the
listing of the graves and the people who were buried here. There
they were, Frank Smith and his wife Julia Etta Smith.
There on the headstone beneath the snow was the first solid piece
of evidence that little baby Juliette who's mother died in childbirth
with her younger sister when she was 3 only years old. On her
birth certificate her name was Juliette Ames. On her head stone it

was...remove the snow...Julia Etta Smith. Wife of Frank Smith.

It was worth driving 120 miles for and much more. Now I had two pieces of evidence, strong pieces, enough that I continued my journey of discovery.

Was it too much to hope that this was the real Etta who took on the alias Etta Place? Well, I was so intrigued by the possibilities that I took on another member of the Wild Bunch possibility and another ghost's family who were told the same thing our family was told, "If I wanted you to know who I am, I'd tell you who I am."

The key to this being a likely accurate match for the people I have been Riding the Outlaw Trail with for 10 years is that they were in Cove, Utah in 1896. Cove is within a few miles of Joseph, Utah. Other significant connections in Joseph, Utah, in 1880 were Joshua Sweat and Bub Meeks...members of the Wild Bunch. They were the baby bunch at this time, but they would grow up, they were cousins of cousins and they were part of Butch Cassidy's Wild Bunch.

The fact that they all had connections to polygamy will open up such amazing avenues of adventure, revealing secrecy designed to save families from the Federalies who were after their polygamist fathers and grandfathers who had fled the United States of America under dire persecutions in the middle of winter while their beloved Nauvoo burned, crossing the Mississippi River on the ice, many babies being born that night in the middle of winter.

I had a second great grandfather, Silas Richards, who was born that night in the woods, they bundled him up and he slept in a drawer from a dresser beside his mother in the woods.

RIDING INTO ROBBERS ROOST

Then out of the clear blue my brother Ross would call and say,

"I have some cowboys who want to take us into Robbers Roost so they can see what we have found. They have horses for us." Unbelievable, the thing I wanted most to experience was riding a horse into Robbers Roost. I had hiked in and out 8 times through the desert, up the sand hills that were 1,000 feet high and making my way through the rugged terrain.

My brother hand Outlaw Trail Adventure partner, D. Ross Nickle, was always there keeping me on task, hiking, getting in, getting out, having what we needed. I was the one taking pictures of everything.

I learned to take pictures while I was hiking to maximize our ability to find really great sites including the inner camp and Etta's Spring below lower pasture. The only problem was I knew how to ride motor cycles, not horses. I asked these seasoned cowboys all dressed for the journey in 1890 boots, hats, tents and gear.

They said wisely, "Don't fall off." I decided that there wasn't a more remarkable way to die than in Robbers Roost so I was willing to take my chances and go for it, following a bunch of seasoned cowboys over the edge down a narrow trail that was the only safe passage down a thousand foot sand hill. More about that later. Did I mention that Bill Long made sure I had all that I needed to make my life work along the way as I rode with him on our Outlaw Trail Adventures? Absolutely remarkable.

And so goes the amazing experiences on my Outlaw Trail adventures.

CHAPTER 8

Butch Was Born In Beaver in 1866

So let's jump back to Beaver, Utah. Butch was born in Beaver, Utah in 1866. He was named after his Grandfather Robert Parker. Now you know Robert Parker even though you don't think you do. Remember the musical Oliver Twist? Based on the book written by Charles Dickens from "bloody" old England. The character of Oliver was patterned after Robert Parker, Butch's grandfather who was a street urchin in London.

Robert Park and Thomas Schofield were both grandfathers of Butch Cassidy. They were both polygamists as well. That's why we are putting these stories here, they are related to Harry Longabaugh is a roundabout sort of way through polygamist families, outlaws, ghosts and DNA, so keep riding, lunch break is over.

Robert Parker Was the Real Life Oliver Twist

Charles Dickens hired a type setter, a relative of Thomas Schofield. Charles Dickens knew Robert Parker as a child and he knew why he was on treacherous and deplorable streets of London. Robert Parker's father and Thomas Schofield's father went in business together. The business failed due to circumstances beyond their control and they were put in the debtors prison which left their families on the streets of London for the year they were in captivity.

Charles Dickens used Robert Parker's ingenuity and will to survive and thrive as a patter for Oliver in Oliver Twist. When Robert Parker and Thomas Schofield went to the harbor to immigrate to America as young men, Charles Dickens came down to the Warf and gave them a signed copy of his new book, "A Christmas Carol". Butch was known to keep that book around all of his life. He was an avid reader and Charles Dickens was his favorite author.

Robert Parker made his way to Utah and settled in Beaver, Utah. He was one of the original 7 families that settled there. He was also a polygamist. He had 3 wives and some of the most interesting in-laws. Ann Hartley was his first wife, the one everyone knows about. Louisa Evaline Lee, daughter to John D. Lee of the Mountain Meadow Massacre fame, and Jensanie Madsen.

This makes Robert Parker son-in-law to John D. Lee and makes Butch grand nephew in law to John D Lee. Which was why Butch was at the execution of John D Lee when he was 11 years old. John D Lee was finally executed in 1877 on the site of the original massacre. Brigham Young fulfilled his promise to John D Lee to protect him until he died. Brigham Young died that year and so it was John D Lee had no more protection and the courts finally caught up with him.

He stayed true to his covenant made oh so long ago under circumstances of such horrendous strain that we have not the wisdom to call it from here. Just be wise when telling stories because there are always more sides to every story. They are usually all mixed together and this becomes the life each of us lives.

So, here we go again. I'm adding the relationship between the person I believe to be Hyrum Beebe whom some believe to be The Sundance Kid and Butch Cassidy. This relationship just happens to pass through John D. Lee. Interesting. Yep, I thought so.

Now, with this chart you can see that Hyrum Beebe as I believe him to be, lived in Circleville, Utah in the same time period as the Parkers were there.

He came from a polygamist family and his father's name was William Albert Beebe who died in Circle, Piute, Utah. The story of he and his 5 wives is another great book for another day.

Anyway, back to John D. Lee. As far as I can find, John D Lee has 18 wives shown on Ancestry.com. This genealogy is not proved out, it is submitted by people who want to share their genealogy. I use the best version that I can find and keep moving.

To prove out any one person takes an enormous amount of time, energy and money. I had limited time, energy and money and so I opted to use what others have left for me as bread crumbs along the way. If you want to prove out any particular piece of genealogy, have at it.

It's all public knowledge on Ancestry or some other public genealogy forum. I had a mission to accomplish and I have stayed focused and true to this mission. Helping the Ghost of the Sundance Kid heal and move into the light. Yes, I know, I just keep moving on this path that keeps opening up and I got to here and can talk to you about all these really amazing and awesome people who have lived marvelous lives of intrigue, profound life lessons, courage, fortitude, creativity. So, let's go with it.

Now, John D Lee and his 18 wives is the best example of a MEGA POLYGAMIST FAMILY. Once you realize that each of his wives has a family and connections it doesn't take long to do the math 18 times siblings of those 18 wives and that's a lot of cousins right there. This is just one family.

Let's ride...Martha Elizabeth Berry, born 22 Nov 1827, in

Nashville, Tennessee was one of John D. Lee's wives.

Margaret Patterson had a sister Agnes Ann Patterson who married Philo T Farnsworth and who's descendants invented the TV. Yes, that modern invention was created from the great stuff here in Utah, Beaver, Utah to be exact. Philo T Farnsworth was also a cousin to Milford Bard Farnsworth who married Rosina, you remember now, "There was A Wedding in Panguitch" in 1892? You will soon enough.

The wedding where Butch Cassidy either met Etta, his first beloved Etta, or got to know her better. They were probably both there since their families were intertwining. In fact, not too long after that wedding there was another wedding. Butch Cassidy's aunt, Eva Clara Bentenson married Cyrus Walter Farnsworth, nephew to Milford Bard Farnsworth who married Etta's sister Rosina in Panguitch that day in 1892, you remember, "There was A Wedding in Panguitch."

This Martha Elizabeth Berry, wife of John D. Lee, was also married to Dennis "Smiling" Dorrity, III. Now "Smiling Dorrity" had 4 wives listed on Ancestry.com one of who was Agnes Ann (twin) Patterson. Now why do we care whether these people are smiling or not? Are you ready? This is it, this is why we came all really care.

Agnes Ann Patterson (Dorrity) and Margaret Patterson (Smith) are sisters. So we have the wife of John D. Lee, Martha Elizabeth Berry, and another of the plural wives of Martha's second husband Smiling Dorrity Agnes Patterson who originally was married to Philo T Farnsworth cousin to Etta by marriage. Anyway, in all the confusion a direct relative of The Sundance Kid alias Harry Longabaugh has a cousin. WOW, who would have thought. His name was John X Smith.

Now John is fascinating because he joined the LDS Church in England and when he did, his family who was fairly well off financially, disowned him. He was about 20 and decided to immigrate to America.

With the help of the couple that converted him, he was able to get passage on a ship and made the trek. He ended up being called to, of all places on the planet, Beaver, Utah. Our Margaret Patterson who we met above married said John X Smith, second cousin one time removed of The Sundance Kid alias Harry Longabaugh.

That's fascinating you say. Yes, I agree. Now, it gets even more fun. I can hear Butch Cassidy riding up now with more to this story. The rest of this story is why I insisted you pay attention to my tale.

I knew you wanted in on this one. I'm not even going to preview it for you, I'm going to let you do the discovery yourself. I'll just give you access to the relationship charts which took me 10 long years and thousands of miles to procure in this form.
Time for a MEGA DRUM ROLL (that was great, you're getting better)

Gasping for breath I woke up from a vision dream knowing there was more than one Sundance Kid and that there were 5 women who used the name Etta. And that you can separate them out but using your intellect and observing which facts go together. Simple Sesame Street game of which of these things is not like the other.

It worked and this is more of what I found.

Relationship: Harry A Longabaugh to Robert BUTCH Leroy Parker

Robert BUTCH Leroy Parker is the 1st cousin 1x removed of husband of 2nd cousin 1x removed of Harry A Longabaugh

2nd great grandparent

Anthony Smith
b: 12 Oct 1765
Hampshire, England
d: 1848
Raunds, Northamptonshire, England

Mary Tinckler
b: 01 Apr 1768
Raunds, Northamptonshire, England
d: 1807
Raunds, Northamptonshire, England

Great grandmother

MaryMHL Smith
b: 02 Jul 1792
Raunds, Northamptonshire, England
d: 06 Feb 1807
Raunds, Northamptonshire, England

2nd great uncle

John Smith
b: 25 Mar 1796
Raunds, Northamptonshire, England
d: 27 Jun 1866
Raunds, Northamptonshire, England

Maternal grandmother

RachelMHL Tuston
b: 1793
Phoenixville, Chester, Pennsylvania, USA
d: 1850
Pennsylvania, USA

1st cousin 2x removed

John X Smith
b: 09 Dec 1827
Raunds, Northamptonshire, England
d: 05 Feb 1905
Beaver, Beaver, Utah, USA

Mother

AnnieMHL G Place
b: 27 Sep 1828
Phoenixville, Chester, Pennsylvania, USA
d: 18 May 1887
Phoenixville, Chester, Pennsylvania, USA

2nd cousin 1x removed

Sarah Smith
b: 22 Feb 1861
Beaver, Beaver, Utah, USA
d: 23 Jun 1932
Beaver, Beaver, Utah, USA

Self

Harry A Longabaugh
b: 19 Apr 1868
Phoenixville, Chester, Pennsylvania, USA
d: 08 Nov 1908
Bolivia

Husband of 2nd cousin 1x removed

Ebenezer Gillies
b: 07 May 1859
Beaver, Beaver, Utah, USA
d: 05 Aug 1944
Milford, Beaver, Utah, USA

Father-in-law of 2nd cousin 1x removed

Ebenezer Gillies
b: 18 Nov 1819
Edinburgh, Midlothian, Scotland
d: 22 Apr 1883
Beaver, Beaver, Utah, USA

This is the Longabaugh half…

Robert BUTCH Leroy Parker is the 1st cousin 1x removed of husband of 2nd cousin 1x removed of Harry A Longabaugh

Grandparent of husband of 2nd cousin 1x removed

John Gillies
b: 05 Aug 1789
Perth, Perthshire, Scotland
d: 1856
Argyll, Scotland

Uncle of husband of 2nd cousin 1x removed

Robert Gillies
b: 12 Sep 1819
Perth, Perthshire, Scotland
d: 06 Oct 1866
Farmington, Davis, Utah, USA

1st cousin of husband of 2nd cousin 1x removed

Annie Campbell Gillies
b: 12 Jul 1847
Perth, Perthshire, Scotland
d: 01 May 1905
Panguitch, Garfield, Utah, USA

1st cousin 1x removed of husband of 2nd cousin 1x removed

Robert BUTCH Leroy Parker
b: 13 Apr 1866
Beaver, Beaver, Utah, USA
d: 1956
Leeds, Washington, Utah, USA

This is the Butch Cassidy half.

Did I shock you? Cool. You'll live. These connections go on and on and on...The Outlaw Trail Adventures Data Base is phenomenal for making these connections between Butch Cassidy, Sundance, Etta and the rest of the Wild Bunch and the MEGA POLYGAMIST FAMILIES and history including George

Washington (President), Thomas Jefferson, Jesse James, etc. These charts tell the story better than any interpretation of information, but we must start somewhere. My Outlaw Trail Adventures Genealogy Database is the solid ground my Ghost Stories stand on. So, now we have the key players to my Ghost stories evolving in your consciousness and you even know about "A Wedding in Panguitch".

You knew how Butch is related to The Sundance Kid Alias Harry A Longabaugh which is really more of an interesting connection than anything else.

I found this connection when I spent over 10,000 hours doing the genealogy research on the Wild Bunch Families supporting the YDNA and MITO DNA testing which we have been doing all these long 10 years. Most of our efforts told us who someone was not. It took a lot longer to prove who they were. Since then, I've quadrupled the time I've spent of the OTADB, chasing Ghosts, Outlaws, Polygamists and DNA. What a ride!

However, we have established a baseline McCarty YDNA marker set, we have established a baseline Longabaugh YDNA marker set, we have Parker YDNA, we Autosomal DNA from the granddaughter of Tom McCarty, Mauvis, we have Autosomal form the Longabaugh family cousins, we have MITO DNA from the Longabaugh Family and can establish with confidence the MITO DNA Harry A Longabaugh probably had.

We have learned that there are always circumstances which make your testing scheme and story lines go a different direction than you originally though. We have others and are working on our latest theories. Some of these we will allow to unfold before your very eyes here in this book about Ghosts, Outlaws, Polygamists and DNA.

Strange mix for an even stranger story.

You have now been baptized by fire into the family systems of the Wild Bunch. Many of you are already cousins whether you know it or not. Be good, or I'll tell you who your relatives are and what they did.

Behold John X Smith lived in Butch's Beaver. John X Smith is a cousin of Harry Longabaugh's mother, just for your information:

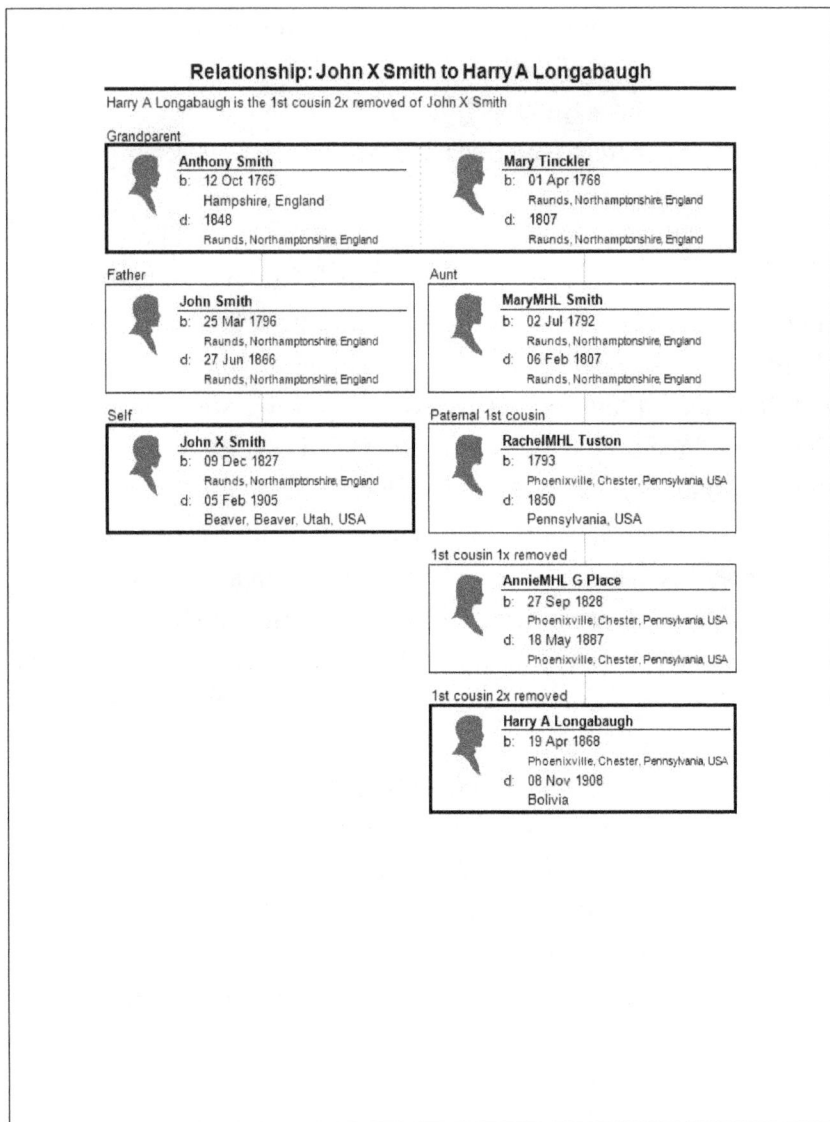

Relationship: John X Smith to Harry A Longabaugh

Harry A Longabaugh is the 1st cousin 2x removed of John X Smith

Grandparent

Anthony Smith
b: 12 Oct 1765
Hampshire, England
d: 1848
Raunds, Northamptonshire, England

Mary Tinckler
b: 01 Apr 1768
Raunds, Northamptonshire, England
d: 1807
Raunds, Northamptonshire, England

Father

John Smith
b: 25 Mar 1796
Raunds, Northamptonshire, England
d: 27 Jun 1866
Raunds, Northamptonshire, England

Aunt

MaryMHL Smith
b: 02 Jul 1792
Raunds, Northamptonshire, England
d: 06 Feb 1807
Raunds, Northamptonshire, England

Self

John X Smith
b: 09 Dec 1827
Raunds, Northamptonshire, England
d: 05 Feb 1905
Beaver, Beaver, Utah, USA

Paternal 1st cousin

RachelMHL Tuston
b: 1793
Phoenixville, Chester, Pennsylvania, USA
d: 1850
Pennsylvania, USA

1st cousin 1x removed

AnnieMHL G Place
b: 27 Sep 1828
Phoenixville, Chester, Pennsylvania, USA
d: 18 May 1887
Phoenixville, Chester, Pennsylvania, USA

1st cousin 2x removed

Harry A Longabaugh
b: 19 Apr 1868
Phoenixville, Chester, Pennsylvania, USA
d: 08 Nov 1908
Bolivia

CHAPTER 9

Etta Is A Utah Cousin, One of Our Own

The Infamous Trio: Sundance, Butch and Etta

How did we get the trio of Sundance, Butch and Etta?

Well, in Wayne County, Utah, in 1890's George Monteville Ames moved into a home in Lyman, Utah. Next door lived Luzernia Ann Allred and Bill Long were direct family relations.

Luzernia's son Hiatt Morrell married Ruby Lazenby. Ruby's father was Walter Lazenby. Walter Lazenby had several children including Ruby with his first wife Mary Cook who then died in child birth in Fish Springs, Utah. Walter then married Nadine Ames, **half sister to Etta**. They all moved from Bicknell to Teasdale to Fish Springs just over the hill. They lived there during a time when ranching cattle and sheep was the wealth of the people.

Ooooooo...turn your head back around, it just went spinning off. That's what I'm say'en...half-sister to THE ETTA. The first Etta, that is. There were several women who used the name of Etta to get around while associated with The Wild Bunch. As I have come to know them, this list includes the first Etta whose real name was Julietta on her birth certificate and Julia Etta on her head stone. But she was the first Etta that Butch fell in love with. Other women in Butch's life that took on the alias of Etta include Anne Marie Thayne, Ann Bassett, Ethel Butchel and others. I woke up from a dream about them realizing that they were separate and distinct individuals. Then all the stories started to make sense.

What better way to hide them all under one name. Same strategy with Sundance, same strategy actually was used with Butch. Hollywood took the combined persona's and made the remarkable movie, "Butch Cassidy and The Sundance Kid." We all fell in love with them all over again, especially Etta on the bicycle with the song, "Raindrops Keep Falling On My Head."

There is a lot more about Etta to come forth. So many connections, such strong circumstantial evidence that you will have the opportunity to wade through it will be fun to see how you calculate the evidences, facts and figures. Let's move on and add some other of the major players in Butch Cassidy's Wild Bunch associations.
So let's put James Allred into the equation. This James according Kerry Ross Boren, took over after Butch went to South America. Robert Leroy Parker (Butch) had a childhood friend in Beaver, Utah, who is a cousin of Luzernia's (wife of The Sundance Kid William Henry Long), James Allred.

You actually know him. He was the bishop in Circleville and Circleville was under siege from the Indians during the Black Hawk war. Early on in the first settlement of Long Valley and Circleville, Utah, there was a massacre and many white people died, including babies. Then the Indian Wars heated up. Circleville residents felt a huge danger, rightfully so.

The Indians were rounded up and taken to the church in Circleville. Some of the braves had their bands loose and were attempting an escape when they were discovered and the order was given to exterminate them...all but the very young children who wouldn't remember.

This was unfortunate and from here, all I can say and may all who ventured into these massacres be able to overcome this darkness and be free to move into a more profound, powerful and loving space. Let's generate a round of courage to be powerful, positive and progress always in all ways.

There had been skirmishes between the settlers and the Indians before in Circleville area, Long Valley, when the Indians attacked and killed women, children, brutally. Some of those who lost their children and spouses in the attack were in Circleville.

The thirst for retribution that could never come, the ever present and real life threatening, presence of the hostile Indians in the area, and the circumstances at the time lends a necessity to survive by attacking a perceived enemy. It's' not mine to judge, how can we judge when we were not there living under siege and threat of war.

So, where is this all leading? James Allred grew up with Butch Cassidy. Reuben Allred was one of the main rescuing team who followed Ephraim Hanks out into the dead of winter to find the Martin and Willey Handcart companies and bring them in. Ephraim got the jump on the rest of them because he had a dream and his guide in the dream asked him to go help and he said yes.

The next day, he was called with the rest of the brethren to go. He said, "I can go now." and he did. Reuben Allred and his group came next with a couple of days and together they got those people off the mountain...saved lives and relieved some very challenging human discomfort.

So here we have an intense time cementing the relationship between the Ephraim Hanks who would eventually settle Hanksville, Utah, and the Allred's, cousins of Luzernia Ann Allred, wife of the Sundance Kid and my second great grandmother. There are other significant relationships which you'd best start keeping track of so you can keep up with our excite'n stories.

Now there is a relationship between Ephraim Hanks and Charley Gibbons. Charley Gibbons generated over a million dollars in wealth 3 times in his life. He ran a station along the travel route from Utah to San Bernardino and other parts in California. Another, George Monteville Ames and Ephraim Hanks and Charley Gibbons connection is very strong, there; gotta be a story here as well. They all got in on the travelers who were on their way to the gold fields in California that needed food and lodging.

ELLIS EAMES, ETTA'S GRANDFATHER

There was a man who joined the Mormon Church early on named Ellis Eames. He was half owner of Hahn's Mill. The same mill where the Hahn's Mill Massacre took place 31 Oct 1848 after Governor Boggs of Missouri issued an extermination order focused on exterminating the Mormons.

Ellis Eames barely escaped with his life. There was a bullet hole in the tail piece of his coat jacket. His wife gathered their children and headed into the woods and was fortunate enough to find cover and stay protected through the siege. It was a dark time in history.

Why do we care about Ellis Eames at this time? Well, well, well...you may want to put him on your maps and pull out your genealogy charts. For his granddaughter was the first Etta in Butch Cassidy's life. 1894 to 1896.

This is a huge claim and by the time I weave my tales together, you'll understand and see how remarkable a story this really is. Etta is a Utah girl. Now, there are several women who were associated with The Wild Bunch. Each taking on the Etta persona which kept them all safe and made the tells much more interesting.

Again, from my research, I can find the following women who took on the Etta name or became a part of the Etta Place mystery.

Will the real Etta Place please stand up:

THE FOUR FACES OF ETTA

Ann Bassett played her part Doris Burton has her covered well in her writings,
Ann Bassett and Butch sat out under a tree in Leeds, Utah writing their memoirs according to Eric the curator of the Leeds, Utah Wild West Museum, this is a must see museum along with the one in Sundance, Wyoming.

Ethel Butchel played her part and was one who was well bred and very much in love with Butch.

Ann Marie Thayne played her part, may well have married Harry Longabaugh alias of
 Sundance and they probably had a son named Harry Longabaugh junior, research
 continues.

Julietta Ames played her role as the first beloved Etta in Butch's life before he went to WY prison. This Julietta changed her name to Julia Etta by the end of her life. She came from a family of musicians who were well known on the community. She was born in 1877. She was 5' 3" short. She was stunningly beautiful. And like her grandmother before her, her granddaughter had an elegant beauty about her. Her home was well appointed yet comfortable. She looked exactly like her grandmother.

I've heard of another Etta possibility, but I'm not convinced she's connected yet. So let's get this story rolling on down the road of history. More about this as we go, Hollywood aside though appreciated.

It is rumored that one of the Blackburn girls would go into the roost. Well, one of the Blackburn girls was also married to the Bub Meeks family, so that would make sense. I'm comfortable with the four faces of Etta's listed above.

Meanwhile,...Well, well, a little in-depth research and I find that a book which had handcart company information was wrong. Just plain wrong. This book says Robert Parker, grandfather to Butch Cassidy, died trying to save his family and friends on the mountain in the Willey and Martine Handcart companies. Not so. He was not in those companies. He came in the one before that.

BUTCH'S FATHER MAX PUSHES A HAND CART WITH MCARTHUR COMPANY

Max Parker was 12 and came across in a hand cart company along with his father Robert Parker. Robert Parker did not die in the deep and treacherous snows with the Willie and Martin handcart companies...he was with the company before that, the McArthur company.

Oh, and he didn't die on the mountain after breaking snow day after day ... bla, bla, bla. He got through with some serious challenges but they beat the winter snows. He didn't even die there, he went to Beaver, Utah and had two more wives sealed to him and more children including a grandson name Robert LeRoy Parker alias Butch Cassidy.

You know, life on the Outlaw Trail is amaz'en...what happened, what likely happened and what may have happened are often confused for the purpose of whoever is tellen' the tale. Tales and folk lore are the really great stuff life is made out of. I wouldn't change any of it. What good is a tale about the campfire in the evening if it's not excite'n'?

The Outlaw Trail is the grandest of adventures into history, into families, into polygamy, into the Wild West at its finest, Utah style. And of course, the only really great road map is...ta dah...genealogy charts, pedigrees that is, local history, old pioneer cemeteries, lots of figuren' and a little bit of blood, sweat and tears searchen' for stuff.

With the intoxicating prospect of becoming wealthy like Robert Redford catches up with most of us while riding the Outlaw Trail. Heck, everyone has their romantic beliefs about the beautiful and mysterious Etta.

I'm here to tell you straight up that it's even better then you've ever imagined. Wilder a tale than is allowed to be told yet, and twists and turns through the Civil War, through Jesse James and Cole Younger, through the Hahn's Mill Massacre on Shoal Creek in Missouri on that fateful Halloween Night 31 October 1848.

Weaving a web of evidence which leads us to the understanding that if our Etta isn't THE ETTA then she should be according to Hollywood. (Snicker, snicker) If our Sundance Kid isn't THE MAIN SUNDANCE KID, then he missed the greatest opportunity to be so.

Howbeit, he is the main Sundance Kid as far as I can tell since he's

married to Etta and Sundance's **alias is Frank Smith**, two strong evidences,

very strong evidences.

I'm convinced William Henry Long also played a major role in the tales of the Sundance Kid. They are related through marriage even, not to each other of course...
But there was another...

You want connections? I'll give you connections. Watch this!

ETTA: ROSE OF THE DESERT, QUEEN OF THE NIGHT

Etta: Rose of the Desert, Queen of the Night and her heritage. She's a Utah girl.

With the following research and connections, I became absolutely convinced that Julia Etta Smith was indeed Etta. The first Etta. The Etta that Butch Cassidy fell in love with, danced with in Milford, Utah, and developed a lifelong friendship with.

She was young and very beautiful. She was already a handful

for her father who threatened to disown her if she kept seeing those guys. She was a wild one. She was Etta, Rose of the Desert, Queen of the Night.

By 1894, Butch Cassidy went to prison in the Wyoming Territorial Prison for 2 years. By the time Butch had returned, Julia had met and married Frank Smith. She met him on the train to Cove. Cove, Utah was the final stop on the railroad line past Richfield, Utah for about 4 years. After that, they put the railroad through to Marysville. The 4 years between the time Frank Smith rode into the Cove on the first train down that line and stayed at the boarding house that Julietta Ames was working at and 1900 when Etta and Sundance went to South America were filled with interesting connections.

Here is how I put the pieces together: Following the bouncing ball and remember, don't swallow the ball!

Now this is how 10 years of research look somewhere in the middle of my research first for William Henry Long and then for Julietta Ames who married Frank Smith. Here's the breakthrough that put the pieces together for the first time.

A report of the Ames/Parker connections:

Sarah Angelina Ames (sister to George M Ames)

Married David Alma Losee

Children in Orderville, Kane, Utah

Olive Losee   31 Jul 1878 Orderville, Kane, Utah

George Alma Losee   06 Dec 1880 Orderville, Kane, Utah

Rebecca Losee   19 Aug 1883   Orderville, Kane, Utah

Isaac Huff Losee 11 Nov 1884 Panguitch, Garfield, Utah

John Losee   11 Mar 1886   Cannonville, Garfield, Utah

Isadora Losee   12 May 1889   Cannonville, Garfield, Utah

Apelona Losee   31 Jul 1890 Panguitch, Garfield, Utah

Ephraim Losee   13 Nov 1893 Panguitch, Garfield, Utah

Fannie Losee   19 Nov 1896 Panguitch, Garfield, Utah

Sarah Angelina Ames is sister to George Monteville Ames

Isaac Losee and Sarah are in Orderville, Kane, Utah in 1880 census as well as Eliza Jane Losee who had a child in Orderville. Her husband is Orville Sutherland Cox, 1859, Fairview, Sanpete, Utah.

This puts Julia's aunt, Sarah Angelina Ames, sister to her father, George Monteville Ames, living in Orderville, Kane, Utah, in 1880 with her husband Isaac Huff Losee and her daughter Eliza Jane Losee who is married to Orville Sutherland Cox.

ETTA IS RELATED TO BUTCH

Significance: **Butch Cassidy moved with his family in 1879 from Beaver, Beaver, Utah to Circleville.** If this is close to Orderville, then we have JULIA ETTA's aunt in Orderville 75 m from Parkers with Bentensons and Panguitch in-between.

Sarah Angelina Ames sister to George Monteville Ames and her husband and family are in Panguitch, Garfield, Utah 1890 through at least 1896 when Apelona, Ephraim and Fannie are born.

SIGNIFICANCE: George Monteville Ames and Mary Callahan are there, likely with Rosina and Julia at the same time because Rosina married Milford Bard Farnsworth in Panguitch, Garfield, Utah. And George Monteville Ames, father the Julia Etta, disowned her for hanging with the wrong crowd at the dances in Milford.

James Orvel Ames in born in Panguitch, Garfield, Utah in 29 Jan 1892

Rosina and Milford Bard Farnsworth were married 22 Apr 1893 in Panguitch, Utah.

Isaac Huff Losee was born in Panguitch, 11 Nov 1884 which puts his mother Sarah Angelina Ames Losee, sister to George Monteville Ames in Panguitch, Utah, then Cannonville, 33.5 miles away by Tropic, Utah, then back to Panguitch for the last 3 children from 1890 thru 1896 and then Sara Angelina Ames died in Panguitch in 1899.

Who is in Panguitch 1892-1893?

George Monteville Ames 1884, 1890-1899

Mary Callahan 1884, 1890-1899

Rosina Ames 1892, 1893

JULIA ETTA 1884, 1892, 1893,

Other Ames children

Sarah Angelina Ames (aunt to R and JULIA ETTA) (died in Panguitch1899)1884, 1892 thru 1899)

In 1896 Mary Nadine Ames, half sister to R and JULIA ETTA, daughter to George Monteville Ames, married Walter Lazenby and moved to Loa, Wayne, Utah and lived there until after 1909 and died in Payson, Utah.

George Albert Ames was in Loa, 1907, then Spring Glen 1908 where and when baby Johnny died, then back to Loa and Lyman for many children and years.

Sarah Angelina Ames and her husband Isaac Huff Losee, and their family were in Panguitch 1884, then moved to Cannonville, 33.5 miles to the east near Tropic, Utah, then in 1892 they moved back to Panguitch. George Monteville Ames, Mary Callahan and their family were in Panguitch 1892 and in 1893 Rosina married Milford Bard Farnsworth in Panguitch. Rosina's aunt, Sarah Angelina Ames and her husband Isaac Huff Losee were in Panguitch at this time and she died there in 1899.

David A Losee and his wife Sarah A and wife Mary M with several children each.

David A Losee is son of Isaac Huff Losee and brother to Eliza Jane Losee is also there in 1880 in Orderville.

Orderville, Utah is 73 miles from Circleville, Utah.

Spry is 60.3 miles from Orderville, Utah. Butch Cassidy and his family moved to Spry, Utah by 19 June 1879 because his brother Maximillian Ebenezer Parker was born in Spry on that date.

This puts George Monteville Ames's sister 60 miles from Robert LeRoy Parker and his family in 1879 to 1880.

Beaver is 92 miles, the Parkers had a child there during this time.

1869 to 1894 the Parkers were living from 60 miles to 92 miles away from Julia's aunt.

George Monteville Ames and Mary Callahan are living in Payson until James Orvel Ames in born in Panguitch, Garfield, Utah in 29 Jan 1892. **This is probably why Rosin and Milford Bard were married in Panguitch.** Then Rosamond Martha Ames was born in 1894 in Beaver and 1897 Angus Arwin Ames was born in Blackrock Millard, Utah. This by 1901 Elva and Eba were born in Torrey.

George Albert Ames, brother to JULIA ETTA, had a son George Albert Ames born 03 Dec 1908 in Spring Glen, Carbon, Utah who died 1909 in Spring Glen.

This puts Rosina and her brother George Albert Ames in Spring Glen when Baby Johnny died and was buried by friends in a borrowed grave. Steven Martindale Farnsworth, brother of Milford Bard was living there as well.

Bertha Elvira Anderson, daughter to Sarah Elvira Meacham, JULIA ETTA's cousin sister who married Carl Christian Anderson (I believe this is where Mary Anderson (name used by Etta as alias in outlaw world0 AND where the name Mary's Resort used at Robbers Roost all came from...Sarah Elvira Meacham was caring for baby Johnny and JULIA ETTA was going by Mary Anderson as an alias).

Anyway, Bertha Elvira Anderson was born in Joe town, Beaver, Utah 31 Jul 1896. This puts Sarah Elvira Meacham (Bertha's mother), Cousin-sister to JULIA ETTA in Beaver during the time Julia and her father were between Beaver and Blackrock. By 1897 JULIA ETTA had moved to Joseph and was living taking care of Rosina's children and working at a boarding house. Bertha Elvira Anderson married Charles Leroy Dalton born 25 Mar 1892 in Montpelier, Bear Lake, ID., I believe Luzernia's female relative, cousin of some sort also married him. Out of Hatch UT. He is 10th cousin 2x's removed from the Dalton Gang, not significant, but interesting.

The Meachams are in Beaver 1896. Daughter Bertha Elvira Anderson married A Dalton. Sarah Elvira Meacham and Charles Christian Anderson cousin-sis to JULIA ETTA were in Joe Town, Beaver, 1896, Diamond Juab, Utah 1898 and Lake Shore, Utah by 1900, Payson by 1904 and back to Eureka, Juab by 1906.

Rosina and Milford Bard Farnsworth were married 22 Apr 1893 in Panguitch, Utah. Rosina's father, George Monteville Ames and Mary Callahan had children in Panguitch in 1892, so the Rosina and JULIA ETTA were likely in Panguitch in 29 Jan 1892 when their brother was born.

Rosina married Milford Bard Farnsworth 22 Apr 1893 I Panguitch, Utah, where they were likely living at the time with father Milford Bard Farnsworth and his second wife, their step-mother Mary Callahan.

These are the significant connections, piece by piece, which connected the dots and created a clear picture of the fact that this Julia Etta Ames is in fact the first Etta that Butch fell in love with and danced the night away in Milford, Utah for 2 years.

This same Etta moved to Joseph, Utah and was working at the boarding house in Cove, Utah, when the first train came into The Cove and the handsome Frank Smith swept her heart away. They were married in Loa, Utah in 1896 just in time to go into Robbers Roost with Butch.

THE WHO'S WHO OF WILD BUNCH COUSINS

By 1895 Etta's sister, Rosina, who's brother-in-law Cyrus Walter Farnsworth married Butch's aunt Eva Clara Bentenson. Rosina and Milford Bard Farnsworth were having a child in Beaver Bottoms 16 Mar 1895. Then by 1896 they were in Joseph having Leonard Farnsworth. Then in 1900 they were in Tintic, Utah having Rosina. Then Joseph for Myrtle Von Farnsworth, then 1910 Milford B Farnsworth was born. Then two others, find their birth places.

Since Sharlet Wells said Julia was living in Joseph, helping Rosina with her children while working at the boarding house, it makes sense according the family group sheet which shows their first child George Stevens Farnsworth born 16 Mar 1895 in Beaver Bottoms, Iron, Utah.

This makes it likely that Rosina and Milford Bard Farnsworth were in Beaver Bottoms with George Monteville Ames and Mary Callahan and the JULIA ETTA were with the family. Then in 1897 George and Mary had children in Black Rock and Rosina and

Milford Farnsworth had moved to Joseph and had a baby, Leonard Farnsworth in 1896.

Since JULIA ETTA was supposed to be taking care of Rosina's children in Joseph, this puts JULIA ETTA in Joseph, Utah in 1896. She was also working at the boarding house which is likely in 1896.

Ellen Sophia Jacobs (husband Collins Eastman Flanders 1814) has brother Oden Goodman/Goodenson Flanders b 1866 in Payson who died 05 Sep 1902 in Junction Field burial, Piute, Utah.

Peculiar close location to Circleville and Parkers. He was in his 30's. He had the son in Cove, Utah in 1897 named Oden Flanders.

So he was in Cove, Utah, 1897, with Butch's cousin's location and it was a small town, and was buried in Junction Field Burial, Piute, Utah. Track this for research. His wife was Born in Junction and her family were the Morrills.

Rosina and Milford were having children in Spring Glen, Carbon, Utah 1907 and 1910 which puts them right where baby Johnny died and when he died.

Baby Johnny was born in 1904 and died in1908. His name was John Thomas Edward Smith. The custom of the time was to name the baby after the first person who came to visit. It is very possible the first person was John Thomas McCarty. The his next middle name was Edward after his father and Smith. He died and was buried in a borrowed grave by friends. His own parents were not there in 1908. That's the time the Sundance Kid was supposedly shot in Bolivia. Just ore food for thought.

Oden Raymond Flanders, son of Oden Goodman/Goodenson Flanders born 01 May 1866 in Payson, Utah, died 05 Sep 1902 Junction Field Burial, Piute, Utah. He was born in Cove, Sevier, Utah 08Jul 1897 and died 25 Mar 1955 when I was almost 2 months old.

His next two siblings were Ralph Frederick Flanders born 10 Jun 1899 in Junction, Piute, Utah and Sara Ella Flanders 22 Dec 1901 in Junction, Piute, Utah.

What does this mean? This is a very close proximity of JULIA ETTA to Robert LeRoy Parkers family in Circleville. 5.5 miles to be exact. Do you think perhaps Oden Flanders b 1866 who died 1902 Junction, Piute, Utah, who is JULIA ETTA's uncle, may have crossed paths from 1897 to 1901 in Junction?

Joseph Woodbridge Cook, B 25 Jun 1871, in Provo, Utah, lived in 1920 in Alunite, Utah, which is same town Fred Levi, Cousin to Butch was living in which may be where Butch spent time in 1920 and at the Bed and Breakfast in Marysville Canyon.

Joseph W Cook's father died in Spry, Utah in 1895 on 24 Feb 1895. This is where Butch's family lived in 1879, and were living just down the road in Circleville.
Cyrus Walter Farnsworth has 3 wives. The 3rd wife is Della Morrill who was born in Junction.

Cyrus Walter Farnsworth married to Mary Isabelle Twitchell had children.

CYRUS W FARNSWORTH MARRIES EVA CLARA BENTENSON, BUTCH'S AUNT

So: Cyrus Walter Farnsworth, JR. is married to Eva Clara Bentenson. Her father is Joseph Arthur Bentenson. His first son is Joseph Adelbert Bentenson who married Lula Parker, Butch's sister.
SO:

Mary Isabelle "Bell" Farnsworth in1880 was in Joseph, 1900 in Grampion and Milford in 1900. Cyrus died in Junction, Utah in 1894 and is not in the census. Son Cyrus Farnsworth is in Milford 1900.

William Hamilton Packer's father was born in Uwchlan, Chester, Pennsylvania, 1764, which is located 11.2 miles from

Phoenixville, Chester, Pennsylvania where the Longabaugh family resided. During this time period. Haven't established any familial ties as of yet, however, the location and proximity of the Longabaughs to the Packer families is worth of our best research.

Mary Isabelle "Bell" Tidwell Farnsworth has her father listed in Ancestry.com as William Hamilton Packer. Her grandfather, Moses Packer, was born 11.2 miles from Phoenixville, Chester, Pennsylvania, during the time that the first Longabaugh's were likely settling the area.

Henrich Longabaugh or Longabaugh, Germany, had two sons that we know of, Conrad and Balsam Longabaugh. They immigrated to Pennsylvania, where Balsam died in 1788, which is the first date I can find for this search. This was 24 years after Moses Packer (William Hamilton Packer's father) was born in Uwchlan, Chester, Pennsylvania (1764).

New first date: Aaron Packer was born in Uwchlan, Chester, PA in 1732. His wife, Ann Phipps was born in 1743 in Uwchlan, Chester, PA. Montgomery, PA is 152 miles from Uwchlan, PA. It is near Williamsport, PA, where Longabaugh family member reside in the Sands lines, the Mito descendents.

What does this mean? Longabaughs and Packers were living in close proximity in Pennsylvania for a substantial time period. Sundance left 1871 or so and ended up in Utah. Moses Packer father of William Hamilton Packer left PA and went to Ohio by 1795, with two children born in PA and the rest in Ohio. William Hamilton Packer was born in Ohio, Smithfield, in 1814.

His first wife had many children in Ohio. His second wife was probably married before and had two children whose last name is Twitchell. Then several more whose last name is Packer. Mary Isabel Twitchell was born in Ogden, Utah in 1858, then a sibling also in Ogden, Sarah Ellen Tidwell. In 1865 Sarah Briggs Allen, his second wife, married him and they had several more children. 1864 they were in St. George, the Leeds, Washington, Utah, then Joseph, Panguitch in 1872.

They were in St. George in 1870's with children and possible connections.

With the first Longabaugh date being Balsam's death in 1788 and the first Packer date being a Packer birth in 1764, it's likely the Longabaughs and the Packers were in the same part of Pennsylvania during the same period of time, looks like a possible 24 years of close proximity. Nothing substantial yet, but worth a look see. RESEARCH!

By 1797 Conrad had a son Jonas in Montgomery, Pennsylvania. In 1822 Josiah Longabaugh, father of Harry A. Longabaugh was born in Montgomery, Pennsylvania. Sundance was born in 1867 in Phoenixville, PA.

Let's try this again:

Joseph Adelbert Bentenson is Butch's sister's husband. (Lula's). This makes him bro-in-law to Butch. His sister, Eva Clara Bentenson married Walter Farnsworth. This makes her Butch's sister-in-law.

So Butch's sister-in-law, Eva Clara Bentenson was married to Walter Farnsworth, who is JULIA ETTA's nephew.

So, Butch's sister-in-law is niece-in-law to JULIA ETTA.

So B's sister-in-law is niece-in-law (in-law) to S.

More: Cyrus Walter Farnsworth was apparently born in 3 places: Joseph, Circleville and Beaver around 1879. NO: Butch's aunt Eva Clara Bentenson

This is the relationship established between JULIA ETTA and Butch

So let's do this again:

Butch's sister Lula's husbands aunt is Eva Clara Bentenson.

Eva Clara Bentenson is Butch's sisters aunt-in-law.

Leave out the law and Eva Clara Bentenson is Butches sisters aunt which would make her Butch's aunt (kind of).

Then you take JULIA ETTA's sister's husband's nephew.

That Rosina's nephew-in-law or Rosina's nephew if you take out the law and that's JULIA ETTA's nephew as well. (sort of, by marriage)

So we have Butch's aunt Eva Clara Bentenson marrying JULIA ETTA's nephew Cyrus Walter Farnsworth.

By our stretch of the imagination scenario: We have Butch's aunt marrying JULIA ETTA's nephew. (in-law's kind of a relationship)

This would make JULIA ETTA's nephew Butch's uncle (leaving out the in-law thing).

It also makes Butch's aunt JULIA ETTA's niece. (again, leaving out the in-law thing).

I believe this makes JULIA ETTA Butch's great aunt.

Follow me here:

JULIA ETTA's niece (leave out the law) is Butch's aunt.

So in a very roundabout way:

Butch is kind of JULIA ETTA's great nephew in a close familial sort of way leaving out the whole in-law thing which is significant but not excluding of this scenario.

Again: Once wasn't enough?

JULIA ETTA's niece is Butch's aunt. This makes JULIA ETTA

Butch's great aunt.

JULIA ETTA

Niece

Butch

Or

Butch

Aunt

ETTA

They said they were related...

VOILA!

Read it and Weep!

Oh, by the way, there's a suggested proximity for the Longabaugh ancestry to have crossed paths with the fam-damily here. Nothing in marriage relationship yet, but remote possibilities, just in case you need another adventure in pattern matching and all night with ancestry.com sessions. And there's still the Losee/Butch connection to recreate in Circleville.

In the Grampion, Utah, 1900 at Squaw Spring, Beaver, Utah, the census has Walter Farnsworth with his mother Bell and some siblings. I found this one early on but couldn't prove this was the same Walter Farnsworth who married Butch's sister's aunt-in-law Eva Clara Bentenson. It got put on hold until further light and knowledge came through.

It's been quite a while and finally today it came through and it's a match, while I was look for the other connections. This was a pleasant and tremendous surprise with another gift of possibility with the Pennsylvania connection by location between

Longabaughs and Parkers.

The remarkable census points:

1880 Payson found Julia Etta

1860 Fort Ephraim connect Julia Etta to Luzernia

1900 Grampion connected Julia Etta thru Farnsworth's to Butch, along with Sundance alias Frank Smith to Butch through JULIA ETTA.

And so the research went for these wondrous 10 years. My files are full of these connections and many more like them. With 60,000 names in my Outlaw Trail Adventures genealogy database and 30,000places, many mysteries began to reveal themselves. Including The Baby Bunch at Fort Ephraim in 1860. This was another shocker, but we'll get to Fort Ephraim soon enough.

Oh, something to chew on while we're getting there...the McCarty Family lived next door in Levan, Utah. That's right, Tom McCarty and his family. Tom was 10 years old in 1860. Let that melt your brain down for a while.

CHAPTER 10

This is Wild Bunch Family Lore
The Next Generation

My Original Calling From The Outlaw Trail
By Bambie L. Reed

5 years old. I had been five years old for a couple of
months. It was early spring and with the awakening of the daffodils
and petunias my young yet highly inquisitive mind had
conversation with my angelic mother which set the remarkable
course of my life on a higher path of consciousness.

This critical choice point came about while I was watching
a western. My father, Jack, had brought home a television when no
one else in town had a TV. Yes, it was the late 1950's and
technology stepped into our home to upgrade our life experiences
in a big way. Gulliver's Travels...the original black and white
movie was being played and all the neighbors came over to watch
this astounding talking box called a TV.

I was devastated when Gulliver woke up and found himself
tied down to the beach by hundreds of small ropes and the
Lilliput's had him under their control. Not because he was

captured, but because the TV suddenly went to white fuzz and dad reported that the movie had gone off the air. I cried for him to get it back, I really wanted to watch the rest of the movie. My young mind needed to know and felt betrayed by an electronic device which could just take it away and mom was saying, "Sweetheart, it's not coming back on right now, maybe it will play again another day." I was devastated and no longer trusted that tv box with my attention.

The next show I took the great risk to watch was an old western. Living in the wild west 100 years after my distant cousin Butch Cassidy had ridden the outlaw trail through my Beloved Wayne County and found solace and safety in the Impenetrable Fortress of Robbers Roost in the San Raphael Swell which was the main hide out for the Wild Bunch and other outlaws, rustlers and polygamists. Yes, I meant polygamists. For over 50 years the United States government and the Mormons had a huge war going on over the spiritual practice of plural marriage.

By the 1890's Brigham Young had been dead for over 15 years having died in 1877, the same year that John D. Lee was executed by firing squad on the actual site where 20 years earlier he participated in the Mountain Meadow Massacre. He was the one who saved the children against the orders of his superiors. The Fancher Wagon Train should not have poisoned the waters as they traveled down the Sevier River through Utah which lead to many dying from poisoned springs including two 19 year old cattle ranchers named Proctor Robison and William Young.

They were tending cattle when the infamous Fancher Party came through and when the wagon train left both young men were extremely sick. The weakest of the two was Proctor Robison. William Young send Proctor Robison on the horse back to Fillmore to get help. Proctor was dead by morning. The town came back to get William. He lived for a week but the poisons were too much for his young body and he also died a hideous, painful death. There are always many sides to every story.

NEWS UPDATE: The Church of Jesus Christ of Latter-day Saints opened up their files and did a major scientific research project. The final outcomes concludes that anthrax was probably the culprit. Anthrax spread by the cattle from the Fancher Party. Likely without their know it.

The Fancher Party had their stories to tell and wounds to nurse. This story started way back in Arkansas and the roots of the Latter-day Saint Church.

One of the men to raise up in the early church was Parley P Pratt who quickly rose through the ranks and became a latter day apostle. Now he wasn't perfect, exactly and why he was taking another man's wife, I don't know. It didn't go well for any of them. He was also often in the middle of conflicts which lead to his early demise. While preaching in Arkansas he was brutally murdered. Everyone knew the murderer...no authority would apprehend nor prosecute the murderer. Nor were the persecutions of the Mormon Prophet Joseph Smith any more kind or fair. The Fancher Party was boasting about having the gun that killed Old Joe Smith in their wagons.

Now, I realize the Fancher Party and their families have the rest of the story and from here, all we can do is retell old stories that turned out poorly the first time. So I encourage all of us to be understanding, realizing that, "Save the grace of God go I there also." let's move on through. I add the stories because they are directly impactful on our key players, especially Etta.

1857 IT WAS A VERY INTENSE YEAR

Now, did the Mormons in 1857, when the Fancher Wagon Train came through, give them any of the much needed food supplies? No. Brigham Young decreed to sell them nothing. This caused much suffering for the wagon train as it traveled from Fort Bridger down through Utah basically following the Sevier River. A relative from the Boren Family in Provo had compassion and sold them some food for the babies and children who were starving and paid a high price for having done so by loosing much of his hard fought for farms and wealth. And so goes life on the frontier.

It is well that we open our consciousness and release all judgments. My guidance for this journey is wisdom from long ago, "Save for the Grace of God, go I there also." We do not know what we would have done in 1857 if the United States Government was marching on our young settlement of Utah to squelch the "Mormon Rebellion" due to reports which largely were unfounded and untrue after we had been kicked out of the United States of America back in Missouri.

Not only were they kicked out, they were burned out, persecuted, and killed in the dead of winter being forced to cross the Mississippi River on the ice carrying what they could with them of all they had...most of their valuables were left behind due to persecutions born from a difference in beliefs and life styles.

These are the people who faced untold hardships and walked across America into the wilderness yet again leaving all they had built, facing the unknown and fierce obstacles before them looking for and fighting for a place to be free and live their lives according to the dictates of their own conscience.

After Govern Boggs of Missouri issued an Extermination Order against the Mormons they marched on Hahn's Mill where men, women and children were living their lives trying to build a community and be productive on October 31, 1848. 150 people exterminated including the half owners of Hahn's Mill Ellis Eames, his wife and first 4 children.

We will hear more from Ellis Eames when we get to Utah and settle Provo where he was called to be the first Bishop and take on two more wives by Brigham Young.

Whatever you might believe about Brigham, his brilliant and powerful abilities to colonize brought his people across vast distances to a wilderness in the middle of nowhere by a lake of salt

as guided by Jim Bridger to build Zion in the Shadows of the
Everlasting Hills. And all of that will unfold as we bring these
mega polygamist families from their roots in the heartland of
American to the Wild and Dangerous West. This was the latest
frontier.

When we think of frontiers we most often think of Daniel
Boone who came out of Pennsylvania and settled on the new
frontier of Kentucky or what came to be known as Kentucky.
Daniel Boone's father was Squire Boone and his grandfather was
George Boone of Pennsylvania. George Boone was the 5th great
grandfather of William Henry Long...my second great grandfather.

Bill Long came into my family's lives just in time to save
my second great grandmother, Zernie as she was called, her
official name was Luzernia Ann Allred. Daughter of polygamist
and leading pioneer having crossed the plains in the same wagon
train with Brigham Young at the age of 16.

His name was Andrew Jackson Allred. By 1870's he came
into Wayne County Utah and settled Rabbit Valley along with
William Wilson Morrell, the Lazenby's, Taylors and others. By
July 12, 1876 Zernie was getting married to Silas Morrell in the
newly established town of Fremont, Wayne County, Utah.

This marriage would prove to have an extensive impact on
all of us for generations and it's still being researched, written
about and documentaries are being made as we speak. And so they
should be and more. Profound, powerful, purposeful living at its
finest. All the good, all the bad and most of us in-between.

So, how did Zernie come to marry The Sundance Kid alias
William Henry Long?

By 1891 Zernie was pregnant with her sixth child. Silas had
built and operated a Saw Mill on the Fremont River where Mill
Meadows Reservoir is now and he had an employee, a black man
who made a serious error while working on a log which caused
Silas to injured his back.

An injury that would begin a miserable disintegration in

health and from which he would never recover and in 3 years he was dead from complications which arose including a subsequent stroke, emphysema and so on. Zernie was so angry she got on her horse and chased him clear to the Colorado border. She came back, he never did. Be that what it was, Silas Morrell never recovered.

Silas got emphysema, had a stroke and began to disintegrate to the point death was stalking him.

Looking to save Silas's life, or at least make his emphysema more tolerable, the Morrell's left Wayne County with three families that left Rabbit Valley in 1891 headed for the Mormon Colonies in New Mexico. The Morrells, the Taylors and the Nelsons.

Polygamy was being hunted down and the polygamists were being harassed, imprisoned and punished severely for their religious beliefs. These men wanted only to be with their families and live their lives but for over 50 years they were hunted down and persecuted. Be that as it may, this was the state of the union in Utah in 1891.

WAYNE COUNTY, POLYGAMY, OUTLAWS AND FEDERALIES

At the entrance to Wayne County the people would post a couple of children to play on the gate across the road that came off of Fish Lake Mountain down into Loa, Wayne, Utah. Their job was to alert the valley if anyone came in they did not know. This would give the polygamists time to escape to safety, this would also give the outlaws in the area time to escape to safety.

Often this place of refuge was in Robber Roost, the same impenetrable Fortress where Butch Cassidy, the Sundance Kid and the rest of the Wild Bunch including Etta spent the winter of 1896 through 1897 after they robbed the Castle Gate Coal Company of their payroll.

A cousin of mine found the old lock probably from the

chest from the Castle Gate Coal Company in the Goblin Valley area. Oh, did I mention that Butch was a local boy born in 1866 in Beaver, Beaver County, Utah and Butch or Robert LeRoy Parker as he was named when he was born had two grandfather's who were polygamists? Oh, yes, Robert Parker his grandfather had 3 wives one of whom was Eliza Snow, sister to the Prophet Lorenzo Snow. Thomas Schofield another Butch grandfather was also a polygamist. Many very fine ancestors that we all share here in Utah.

So Butch had a lot of motivation to protect the polygamists who were living "outside the law" of the times, were being persecuted and unduly prosecuted. Kerry Ross Boren, a descendant from an outlaw related family, talks much in his book, "Butch Cassidy" about the Mormon Underground who protected the polygamists as much as they could be protected.

He says Butch gave 10% or so of all that he stole for 10 years to fund the underground. You know, Etta Place, the female outlaw who ran with Butch Cassidy and the Sundance Kid. Think, "Raindrops keep falling on my head," as song playing as they rode the bicycle somewhere in southern Utah." It was a great movie and we all feel in love with Butch and Sundance all over again. Just remember, Hollywood is Hollywood and tell great stories with hints of truth.

We've all grown up watching Butch Cassidy and the Sundance Kid, the most famous and entertaining of all the westerns and outlaw movies. Well, Hollywood being Hollywood and taking creative license to create the highest value entertainment got some of the story right and missed on most of it, including the 1908 faked deaths of Butch and Sundance in Bolivia...yes they were faked. Dan Buck and Ann Meadows, Ann being a relative of Harry Longabaugh who is reported to be the Sundance Kid in the movie and is one of the four faces of the name The Sundance Kid.

Harry Longabaugh was really a minor outlaw and after he

escaped from the law on the train on their way to Miles City, Minnesota, he was never recaptured. The man the law claimed was Harry Longabaugh when they captured him again was really William Henry Long who was exonerated after spending 18 months in the jail in Gillette Wyoming. See the book by my uncle, Jerry Nickle called, "Bringing Sundance Home."

So let's see if we can keep up with the story and it is unfolding. According to Kerry Ross Boren whose grandfather William Coleman Boren was part of Butch Cassidy's Wild Bunch at least in a supportive role supplying their needs and providing safe passage and safe keeping, Butch Cassidy was funding the Mormon Underground for 10 years keeping the polygamists including two of his grandfather's safe from the United States Government who was seeking to imprison the polygamists.

THE MORMON UNDERGROUND

Of the five Mormon Bishops who ran the underground, John Thayne, was the father of Annie Thayne who ran with the Wild Bunch. Also among the bishops was Butch's uncle by marriage Daniel McMullen who lived in Leeds, Utah and ran a store. This is the same Leeds, Utah were long time friend and probable co-parent of a daughter named Flossie is one Ann Bassett originally out of Brown's Park.

Her powerful and profound story parallels Butch's and they eventually are reported to have spend many happy hours under a tree near the Wells Fargo Office now turned museum there in Leed's. The curator of the Museum, Eric has many a great tale to tell and is an awesome resource on this subject. More on this subject later.

Oh, did I say that well known polygamist and church leader Isaac Riddle who lived in Pine Valley, Utah for a long time stayed in Robber's Roost in the San Raphael Swell upon occasion? He was also step-grandfather to one of Butch Cassidy's sister Lula's

Bentenson aunts who was the third or fourth wife of Isaac Riddle. This is an obscure fact because she had 4 husbands over her lifetime and when one died she was taken in by another for safe keeping. Her last husband was Isaac Riddle, a polygamist who spent time in Robbers Roost for safety upon occasion. And so our story begins to take shape. All genealogy is documented in "The Outlaw Trail Adventures" data base by Bambie L. Reed.

In Utah in the last half of the 1800's we were all cousins, Utah Cousins. If you are really good at math, you can figure out how many cousins you get when grandfather had several wives with many children each. Then consider that these children need spouses and they marry, who? Those who are in their community or the one next door. And so the exponential growth is astounding, but makes a great genealogy trail to follow.

The Outlaw Trail Adventures Data Base has 60,000 people and 30,000 places with hundreds of thousands of dates and connections. The OTA DB provided the substantial genealogical research to prove William Henry Long is Bill Long son of James Long, descendents of the Ware Long Family.

The original data base was established to prove that Bill Long was Harry Longabaugh, the Sundance Kid as portrayed in the movie, "Butch Cassidy and the Sundance Kid." Great movie to grow up watching, especially if you live here in Utah, specifically Wayne County the door to Robbers Roost. Especially if your second great grandfather was a remarkable man, saved the family and the farm which was substantial, and many other amazing things including riding with the Wild Bunch...you know, Butch Cassidy.

Yes, Butch is one of the Utah Cousins I was talking about. What we proved was that William Henry Long is not Harry Longabaugh. We used the latest discoveries in DNA, both YDNA and MITO DNA. Not the same on both counts.

CAUGHT WITH HER SKIRTS ALL DUSTY
TELLING GREAT STORIES

Now a little discussion here about people who have gotten caught up in the dust trail of all this Outlaw Trail Adventure excitement. There was a woman who was originally brought into the scene by Uncle Jerry. She was hired to help him make a documentary. The work began and soon she started to show her true colors and do things that served her and were against what she had promised in a written legal contract not to do. Then she took all she could of the information and wrote 3 books using the data she promised she would not use.

Then she put is all together and started getting way out there and taking money from many family members as they were working to do something. I'm not sure what because they all quit talking to me and I was the one, along with my brother Ross, who found much of the family information which brought this all together. We shared with Jerry, Jerry wrote his book, "Bringing Home Sundance." So, I don't know what is happening out there in the other teams in the family and out of the family, but the books Marilyn Grace wrote are marginal and should be proven out detail by detail. They have great pictures though.

Such a story teller she is. I've learned a lot from her, mostly what not to do, some of what to do better than I have been doing. She is of service to Bill Long and that's the important piece as she brought in things that motivated me to dig deeper and make sure I was right. It was hard, but important. So, we are all better off and smarter.

I know my family is a great family and we will work through this just like we've worked through everything else and be more for our experiences.

Butch was born in Beaver, Utah in 1866. He had two polygamist grandfathers and an uncle by marriage who was one of the 5 bishops who ran the Mormon Underground working to keep the polygamists and their families safe from the federal government through 1900. In 1887 when Utah wanted to became a state and the whole polygamy issue came to a head and then shifted with the manifesto given by Church President Wilfred Woodruff.

There's a lot more to all these stories which we'll delve into should the excitement dictate the call to follow the outlaw trail as it weaves and wangles through time and space, history and families. Utah is our home. We came here from everywhere pretty much.

We all came with the desire to make a better life for ourselves and our families. The west was still wild in oh so many ways and we had courage, hope, faith is things greater than ourselves and a determination to take it on, make it our own and thrive whatever came our way.

Diverse yet united in the passion to live here, undaunted, and we met the test each in our own ways. This part of our story is about the Outlaw Trail with the Wild Bunch and extends forward and back in time to capture the depth of connections to all the players which lead up to the Wild Bunch with Butch Cassidy. It also takes up around the globe, though most of our adventures will focus on Utah.

This remarkable story centered around Bill Long, Wayne County, Robbers Roost, Butch Cassidy, the Civil War, Polygamy, the Mormon Underground, Outlaws, massacres, settling the west, cattle, families, and of course Utah. Welcome to Utah. This is our home. If you choose to come to visit us here, we'll take you on the wildest adventures you can imagine...and ours are based on real life people, places, and events.   My great grandmothers taught me how to treat people when they came to visit. Invite them in, feed them, talk a spell and give them a hand if you can. The most important part was visiting. Telling tales based in truth kept us warm with laughter round many a campfire, binding families and friends together, bridging generations with yarns of facing the

143

adventures found at every turn.

So what does Daniel Boone

Have in common with William Henry Long?

Answer: George Boone III is ancestor to Bill Long and to Daniel Boone

- **5th Great Grandfather to Bill Long**
- **Neighbor to Lienbach Family in PA**
  - **Grandfather to Daniel Boone**

MEET GEORGE BOONE III

Background for this story: William Henry Long's genealogy had a Sarah Boone married to a Jacob Stover. In researching the Boone Family in Pennsylvania, I found that this George Boone, III was Bill Long's 5th Great Grandfather, and a neighbor to the Leinbach (Longabaugh) family it is said, and the 3rd cousin 5 x's removed of Harvey A. Logan, member of the Wild Bunch who ran with Butch Cassidy and died in Montana after killing a man named Sandusky. So, you never know who you are related to until you do the discovery research.

- When the first six children of George and Mary Morgridge Boone were born , the Boones were members of the Church of England and ... When the Boones arrived in Pennsylvania, George Boone IV held a certificate of membership in the Religious Society of Friends at Bradninch and George III brought a certificate from the Quaker meeting at Callumpton which is a town northeast of Bradninch about a mile up the River Culm.

- George Boone III generally has been identified as a weaver, but he apparently had a blacksmith shop in Bradninch. He must have serve d his apprenticeship as a weaver in Bradninch because that town had a la w that only those who apprenticed there could be employed in the community. The cloth made in Bradninch was a kind of serge called Duruy.

- That summer, George III and Mary and their six remaining children traveled the some seventy miles to Bristol on foot and bought passage to Pennsylvania. Their ship sailed on August 17, 1717. After their arrival in Pennsylvania o n September 19, 1717 OS, George III and Mary went to Abingdon, where their married son George lived; they apparently did not join the Quakers in Abingdon.

- After about a month at Abingdon, the family moved to North Wale s Township in Philadelphia County where George Boone III applied for membership at Gwynedd Monthly Meeting: "10-31-1717, George Boone Sr. produced a certificate of his good life and conversation from the Monthly at Callumpton in Great Britain which was read and well received."

- By 1720, the Boones had moved again; George III was described as a resident of Gwynedd when he received a warrant for 400 acres of land in Oley Township on December 20, 1718. The amount of vacant land surrounding the tract suggests that he was among the earliest settlers in the area. Late r George III apparently acquired the vacant land surrounding his original tract and his sons obtained land near to or adjoining him in Oley Towns hip.

- The Boone farm in Oley Township in Philadelphia County was included in Exeter Township when it was set-off from Oley in 1741. The family attended Gwynedd Meeting until August 25, 1737 OS, when a new church was organized as Oley Monthly Meeting on May 27, 1742 OS, and later re-name d Exeter Monthly Meeting.

- In May 1728, trouble arose in the Boone neighborhood between the white settlers and a band of Shawnee Indians from Illinois. A Shawnee brave was wounded in a dispute over some meat and panic swept through the district on a wave of rumors about Indian retaliation. George Boone, who was a justice of the peace, had to intervene when some whites threatened t o kill two Indian girls. The homestead of George Boone III, on Monocacy Creek, is a now an historical site. Having chosen what is now, and no doubt was then, a most beautiful piece of fertile, rolling land, George III built a log house upon i t in 1720. Thirteen years later, having prospered, he erected a larger house of stone nearby, which is still standing.

- Having built the new house, George III refused for some reason to live in it himself, but turned it over to his children and continued to reside in the log house until his death. An old family Bible records the fact that " when Grandfather died he left 8 children, 52 grandchildren and 10 great-grandchildren living, in all 70, being as many persons as the house of Jacob which came into Egypt."

- In accordance with the custom of the Friends Society, no stones mark the graves of George Boone III and his wife, Mary, but a far greater memorial is found in the thousands of descendants who unite in honoring their memory.

- The George Boonc III homestead is a short distance south of Oley Line/Limekiln Post Office on a road between highways 73 and 562. The Squire Boon e homestead is about two miles directly south on Owatin Creek, a tributary of Monocacy Creek. Monocacy Creek enters the Schuylkill River about a mile south of Squire Boone's homestead, east of Birdsboro. Exeter Friends Meeting House is between the homes of George and Squire and slightly to the east on a parallel local road, on land purchased from George Boone I.

• The Leinbach/Longabaugh family lived in Oley and were apparently neighbors to the Boones...the same Boones from whom descended Bill Long and Daniel Boone.

• Boone Family Cemetery and graves in Pennsylvania:

Fun and frivolity are at hand. Here are the relationships between the Logan Family (Wild Bunch Fame), the Boone Family (Daniel Boone, Frontiersman), William Henry Long (my second great grandfather-step). Kerry Ross Boren says the Lienbach Family (Harry Longabaugh's ancestors) lived next door. They certainly wherein the Berks, Pennsylvania area and had the same religious belief systems.

History unfolds before us. Bill Long has a direct relationship with Daniel Boone, the legendary frontiersman. Daniel's grandfather is Bill Long's 5th great grandfather. It this great or what?

Just remember when a stranger crosses your path and you think they may be strange, they are probably your cousin or your cousin's cousin and you just happened to inherit the same DNA. I'm just tellen' ya' now so you'll be ready.

FINDING ROLAND MERKLEY, Grandson of The Sundance Kid

D. Ross Nickle on the left, Roland Merkley Bill's Grandson center, Bambie L. Reed on the Right

Grandson of Bill Long, Roland Merkley, said, "I just want to know who my grandfather is." Thanks for your help, Roland, without you we could not get to where we are now. Here's your grandfather and his whole family. For you and everyone along the way we finish what we came here to do.

It was Roland when he was 6 years old that he found his grandfather, William Henry Long, dead on the wood pile from a gunshot wound to the head. Every day Roland would deliver a quart of milk to his grandma and grandpa, Bill and Luzernia Long.

Roland was one of the original descendents who gave us permission to dig up Bill Long and get DNA testing done so we could finally prove who he was. It was a year later that Roland died and was buried next to his grandparents.

Thanks Roland, your love and respect for your grandfather was a great motivator to continue our long and arduous journey to here. Your part was invaluable and helped a great deal to finally get the proof we all desired.

LEWISTON, IDAHO

An old picture of Lewiston, Idaho. Bill Long and his family settled just over the border in Washington on the Asotin Plateau. Many of his siblings settled in the Lewiston, ID area including Mary Mahalia who married James Brammer and eventually ended up in Canada.

DANISH MEADOWS, UTAH, 2008

Bill Long and Luzernia had a cabin in Danish Meadows. It is said in family lore that when they moved from Wayne County around 1917, Bill Long took off for a day and went up Danish Meadows direction. He came back with a bag of gold and bought the property in Duschesne.

Well, my pardoner on the Outlaw Trail, my brother Ross, we went adventuring and proved out the Lore. The "footprint" of the original cabin is still there...vague but clearly identifiable by Ross Nickle who was shown the location by our grandmother, Luzernia

Jackson Nickle Baker around 1970.

There was a metal stove there, handmade in a local metal shop by the blacksmith, may well have been Jeremiah Jackson, son-in-law to Bill and Luzernia. He married my great grandmother, Chloe Morrell. The was a pure white flint piece on top of the stove which had been made into an arrow head by Indians many moons ago and had been fired.

I knew in my heart that when I found the same type of stone, white and fired, I would likely find a place where Luzernia had been and brought this back to the Danish Meadow Cabin...I found the same white stone in only one other place. Lower Pasture in Robbers Roost. Luzernia did deliver supplies into Robber's Roost for Charley Gibbons from his store in Hanksville, Utah.

It may well have been brought to Danish Meadow by Bill Long or Luzernia. It is exciting to image the possibilities of who put that arrow head there for me to find so many years later.

THIS IS WILD BUNCH FAMILY LORE THE NEXT GENERATION

DIGGING UP BILL LONG'S BONES

William Henry Long...In the beginning we all shared a love for Bill Long

and an excitement about who he was...the family lore has always been our family's life blood

and now it has taken on new life through our shared passion for Bill Long's story.

The **First** Exhumation September 2006

By D. Ross Nickle

As a very young boy, my grandmother, Luzernia Jackson Nickle Baker, would often take me to see Viola, Bill Long's daughter, in Midvale, Utah. A common subject in their conversation would be finding Viola's father's family. Eventually, my sister Bambie and I took up the search that has spanned more than 4 generations.

Our objective was, and has always been, to find the true but hidden identity of William Henry Long. Amazing stories were told to me, among these were how "Uncle Bill" was a gunman of the Wild Bunch, the consequence of which forced him to spend the rest of his life covering up who he really was.

We searched long and hard for Bill Long's family in vain. Finally, my sister and I realized we needed some stronger tools to work with and decided to obtain Bill Long's DNA. Our only objective was to get a piece of bone for obtaining this DNA. We obtained the proper signatures and permits and exhumed the body in September of 2006. After the exhumation, we took the femur bone of Bill Long to Sorenson Genetics for testing.

The initial test at Sorenson Genetics only produced a limited amount of Y-DNA with the explanation that the specimen was relatively old and deteriorated. We felt we were at the end of our search, considering the lack of information the testing produced.

About a year later, Sorenson Genetics called and informed us he had new technology for testing old bones and asked if we would be willing to try for a new mitochondrial test on the same bone. This produced a full mitochondrial sequence. We then compared the results against a McCarty mitochondrial live descendent. However, the results were inconclusive.

At this time we began a ***Wild Bunch DNA data base*** with the hope of eventually finding the true identities of these characters. Shortly thereafter, Jerry and his group contacted us and asked if we would allow them to re-bury the bones with a promise of encasing them in a vault, all the while filming the re-burial for his documentary.

We agreed under certain conditions, that they would re-bury Bill Long's bones completely without taking any samples for DNA testing. They agreed. We brought the bones to Sorensen Genetics for the safe keeping of the bones and to oversee the event.

The producers of the documentary contacted me and asked to see the bones. My wife and I met with Michael Carr, Marilyn Grace and their associate at Carl's Jr. on 2100 South in Salt Lake City. They were fascinated by what they saw. At his request, I later met with Mr. Carr in South Jordan. I asked him what they would do if the results we received from Sorenson's came in as a "NO" or inconclusive.

He told me emphatically that he would do whatever it took to discredit our exhumation. That is when both I, and my sister Bambie, decided to distance ourselves from the documentary and no longer contribute to it, although, some of the pertinent information contained in the documentary was obtained through our research.

That same day we went to Sorenson Genetics to obtain the DNA results and met with Tim K. I told Tim about our meeting with Michael Carr and his intentions. I then asked him, " if I handled the bones, would that mar or damage the results?" It was his professional opinion that the bones that were brought in had given a good sequence. He was very confident that the lab was able to get accurate results from the bones. He, however, could not guarantee that this particular human bone belonged to William Henry Long as he was not at the exhumation.

Nonetheless, we do know where the bones came from as we videoed the exhumation and had several witnesses. The video confirms the correct grave site and also the removal of the femur.

The femur was measured at 47 cm long. According to a formula to determine height, which includes allowing for age, Bill Long was 5 ft. 6-3/4" in height. According to experts, using the femur bone is a very accurate way to determine the height of a person. We also measured the rudimentary wood box used for a casket. It measured 5 ft 6 inches inside measurement.

NOTE:

The following paragraph was originally posted to our web page. With the assistance of DNA testing we have concluded that Bill Long is not a McCarty nor a Longabaugh. Bill Long is Bill Long whose father was James Long and they are descendants of the Ware Long family lines out of Culpepper, Virginia, England and before that Germany.

[It has been our opinion that William Henry Long could be either Tom or Bill McCarty, the famous Delta Bank robbers. In fact, according to Salt Lake Police Department records, Bill McCarty measured 5 ft 6 inches and Tom 5 ft. 7 inches in height. Historians agree that Harry Longabough was around 5 ft 10 inches. The son of Tom McCarty, Fred, and either Bill or Tom, died in Delta on that fateful day.

However, one of them escaped, wounded, but "never to be heard of or seen again," according to most historians. Although, maybe, just maybe, he showed up somewhere else, like in Wayne County, Utah, changed his name to protect himself and married a widow with a brood of children. But alas, the proof in the cow pies says: Bill Long is not a McCarty nor a Longabaugh, **he is in fact a Long**.] END OF NOTE

In our research we have found evidences that other Wild Bunch members exchanged identities to cover up who they were and even helped each other get out of jail. We found that William Henry Long used the identity of the Sundance Kid. This tactic worked so well, that it not only fooled the law in his day, it also misled his community and even his family; years later historians are still baffled.

The question needs to be asked: a 27 year old outlaw come into Wayne County and marry a 38 year old widow with 5 children (as in Harry Longabaugh's case)? [And the proof in the cow pies said: not a match.] Or, is it more likely that a 44 year old outlaw, wounded, tired of his outlaw past and desperately seeking refuge from the law marry a 37 year old widow with 5 children?"

That's what we went with and we proved it incorrect. [And the proof in the cow pies said: not a match.] And then we found that Bill Long is Bill Long [The proof in the cow pies said: MATCH 15/15] and he ran with the Wild Bunch, not as Tom McCarty, not as Harry Longabaugh but as The Sundance Kid.

To be successful in overcoming this mystery, an expanding data base of descendents could unlock the scientific proof of the identities of these outlaws that were expert in covering up who they really were.

In the 1990's, Ann Meadows, Dan Buck, Clyde Snow and others traveled to Bolivia and exhumed the bones of two banditos from the states. In this process, they used a live Longabough mitochondrial descendent to compare DNA to. That sequence belonged to Dr. O. Frazolle Edwards, now deceased. They also exhumed the bones of Harvey, Harry's brother in Massachusetts.

They determined that it was likely that Mr. Edwards was related to Harvey, although, Mr. Edwards was not related to the banditos. We were able to obtain exclusive rights from Mr. Edward's descendents to obtain that sequence. We then compared Mr. Edwards sequence to William Henry Long and found that they were also not related.

We have found that the process of matching DNA to scientifically prove identities of outlaws from the past is extremely elusive, if not impossible. We are gathering information for a data base of DNA for Wild Bunch outlaws. The process of gathering these DNA sequences, and compiling this information, has been difficult at best considering the many generations we need to trace, not to mention the introduction of divorce, adoption and adultery which, in many cases, render the results inconclusive.

We have had some success with obtaining both Parker and Longabough sequences and are excited and grateful that this has lead to positive identification of Wild Bunch outlaws now and hopefully more in the future.

On behalf of some of the direct descendents of William Henry Long, we are grateful to see all his bones returned to their rightful place to remain there hereafter. The final Funeral and re-internment was attended by many, many descendents of both the Long Family and the Morrell Family and others who had and interest. Healing the family has begun, Bill Long is happy.

Those attending the 2006 exhumation: D. Ross Nickle, Bambie Reed Zeddis, Abraham F. Nickle, Gaylen Robison, Mike Jenkins from the City of Duchesne and representative of Hullinger Mortuary in Roosevelt, and a representative from the City of Duchesne came to check papers for accuracy.

D. Ross Nickle

THE ILLUSIVE 70 YEAR OLD PINE BOX

It is with deep humility I express my feelings about this whole process. It was the most touching and sobering moment when we found Bill Long's pine box and opened the lid. I felt so strongly that I needed to take this path yet at that moment so many things flooded my consciousness.

All I know for sure, was that this was the path I needed to be on to go where I felt so strongly I needed to go. I apologize for the impact on others. I knew no other way to get to where we are now. And so it goes in life sometimes. Choices aren't exactly easy or clear cut oft times. I did my very best to accomplish what I believed I came here to do. And so it is.

That old pine box was buried deep, much deeper than anticipated. The head stone was a foot or two to the right of the casket. There were fear based tales of the old cemetery being flooded and caskets being misplaced. Concern over whether the remains would be viable due to water damage. So many things that had to be faced and overcome. However, my constant companion in who's honor I walked this path, was always with me during these times.

Oft time it was Bill and I watching from a distance all the goings on. All I knew for sure was how important it all was to him. How important each one of us are to him and Zernie. He was the only grandfather the Morrell children knew.
  Bambie L Reed

Bill Long's Sister's and The Sisters Picture

Ross visited Sherma Payton and she called her sister who was gracious enough to reveal the location of the picture of Bill Long's sisters. We came to believe this picture had been lost to the family, probably burned up in the fire at Bill and Luzernia's two story house. Not so. A copy of it still existed and had been hid to keep it safe for all these years. Our relief and joy was indescribable.

The kids used to got up and down the stairs singing about the M and M, S and S sisters. Mary Mahalia and Sarah Salina.

Sherma Payton gave Ross permission to use this picture for whatever purposes he deemed important. She trusted him to use it well. When Jerry was filming his documentary, Ross and I discussed this and decided to let him know about this picture and the Viola Letter and Sherma Payton who gave the original copy to us.

Because of the significance to the Bill Long story and to promote the family we let Jerry know about them and about Sherma Payton. We gave him permission to use them in his documentary if it served the purposes of telling the Bill Long story.

We share this picture and the Viola Letter both page one and page two which lists Bill Long's father James Long, his mother Ann and all of his siblings. This letter is the final proof that the Y DNA 15/15 match with the Ware Long Family descendants and the census records of a James Long, his wife Ann and their children, all of whom are listed in Bill Long's letter...exactly as the census show.

I had found the original census in 1880 with James Long and his children. His wife Ann Harvey Long had died that year. I found it early on and no one believed it could be them because Jerry's still believed him to be a Longabaugh and Ross and I still believed him to be a McCarty. We had no reason to believe he had come to Washington, yet. When Uncle Jerry hired the genealogist to do the Long genealogy, he found it again and this time, armed with Bill Long's Y DNA they pieced together the Long Family pedigree charts that proved William Henry Long was William Henry Long, son of James Henry Long and Ann Harvey Long. Now it was on solid ground. The Proof was in the Cow Pies!

This is the definitive proof we came to find. We share it here with much gratitude and appreciation, excitement and interest.

Meet Bill Long's sisters Mary Mahalia and Sarah Salina.

Bill Longs Sisters 4 of 7 from original
Do not Duplicate without permission
D. Ross Nickle

Viola's Letter, Our Guiding Light

Viola Long Letter about
her father Bill Long

page 1 of 2 ©2010 Ross Nickle

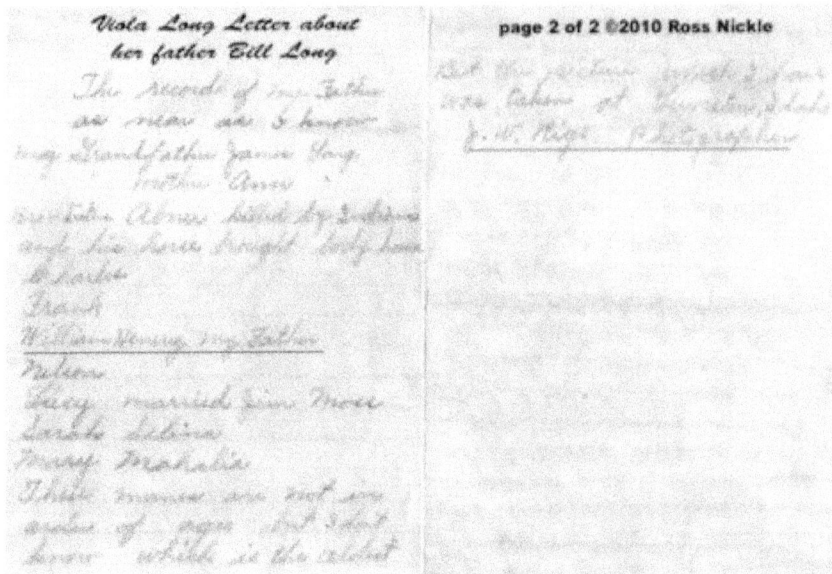

Viola Long Letter about her father Bill Long

page 2 of 2 ©2010 Ross Nickle

(c) 2010 D. Ross Nickle

The pure joy of finding the Bill Long's sisters picture after all these years and miles is so thrilling and to this day I a very, very grateful it came our way so we could share it with the family once again.

Long, not a Longabaugh, he is in fact Bill Long with Y DNA matching the Long Family surname.

HEAVEN IS REAL, THE MOVIE

"Heaven is Real" a deeply touching movie that was recently released helped my soul heal. It has been a long journey through much turmoil as I pursued my highest path following Bill Long through the Outlaw Trail Adventures of a lifetime so he could heal and move into the light.

He and his family, it was important that his family also be free to move into the light. He wished that the example of living he set for his descendants be cleared, express and honored for the remarkable things which were accomplished and the incredible lessons of life he left for all of us.

As the 4 year old in the movie began to talk about his excursions into Heaven while his body lay near death on an operating table. His experiences were all right in line with what I've experienced. I do not need validation of my spiritual experiences for myself, yet others will benefit more once they have their own validation of these things.

This can be so for each of us if our heart and minds have the strength to desire, seek and have the courage to receive our own connections to spirit. Much is here for all of us, most of which we leave on the table of life gifts which God has given to all of us.

Alas, this is an opportunity to come to understand more about ourselves and the universe we all live in. I encourage each of us to go forward, embrace our highest selves and take on the real life experiences we are so fortunate to enjoy.

PROOF OF HEAVEN

And the best yet story that strengthens and augments mine came from an incredible man I met while in Las Vegas last week at a Remote Viewing Conference. He was the Keynote Speaker. His book, "Proof of Heaven" tells of his incredible journey through a NDE, Near Death Experience.

The thing that makes his story to outstanding and worth of our highest consideration it that he is a neurosurgeon and the solid science medicine that was used with him when he was in a 7 day coma from rare form of bacterial meningitis. His story is above reproach of the usual dogma and critics. It's a must read story so you can better understand the stories I am sharing with you're here. His name is Dr. Eben Alexander.

CHAPTER 11

An Outlaw Chooses to Heal, Moves Into the Light

TO HEAL AN OUTLAW BY BAMBIE REED

What does it take to heal and outlaw?

You have no idea! I would not have believed it all except that I was on the front lines. And sometimes that included being under heavy fire from all directions, some of them unknown sources. This I had not anticipated, yet the growth of understanding that came out of it was worth the fight to survive.

It takes a 5 year old in 1960: When I was 5 years old I saw a western on TV which was actually fairly new to the world, and I wanted to be the preacher who helped the people, actually healed them and helped them...not the other fire and damnation preacher who took all the people's money and left them with guilt and shame and a condemn God.

It takes 12 years of research from 2002 to2014: Including the latest in DNA discoveries of Y, Mito and Autosumal DNA which lead me to Rockville, Utah and the old time country doctor and religious man named John James Allred..a Utah Cousin of mine.

It takes an abandoned and haunted old rock 4 story round house in Herriman, Utah in 2003: At Midnight with a digital camera taking pictures of orbs of light, 5 seventeen year old friends wanting to talk to ghosts, a ghost who wanted to heal and move into the light, a 15 year old who just wanted to talk to a ghost all his life, a psychic who came to drive the get-a-way car and supervise the ghost hunt.

It takes one of those Utah cousins of mine and the Outlaw Trail Adventures Data Base in 2012: 60,000 names of relatives of The Sundance Kid, Butch Cassidy, Bub Meeks, Joshua Sweat, Tom McCarty, and John James Allred, a healer, doctor, man of service.

It takes my great uncle Silas LaVerl Morrell and the courage of his daughters Elva and Sherma, and my second great grandmother Luzernia Allred Morrell Long, and my uncle Jerry Nickle, and my brother and pardoner on the Outlaw Trail D. Ross Nickle, and Joel Frandsen, Robbers Roost, the Blackburns, the Taylors, the horses, the cousins...the descendents, in short the whole famdamily. Like I said, in Utah in the late 1800's we are all family, cousins to be more precise. And that's just where it begins.

And most importantly it takes a ghost in 2003: Who once road the Outlaw Trail who wants to heal and move into the light coming to a second great granddaughter at a haunted old rock 4 story round house in Herriman, Utah in 2003 who when asked what he came to us that night for said, "I lived a long harsh life. I have experience some very hard things. I'm now ready to heal and move into the light. Will you help me?"

It takes digging up Bill Long's bones (3 times) and re-internment (4 times) with a funeral in 2011: Bill Long's second funeral in his life or death process to be more accurate. It takes a risk or two and a disruption or two in the family relationships which have been strained time and again, but that's nothing new, just uncomfortable for a while and sad. Hopefully, when this all comes together we come away more than we ever thought we could be as a family and as individuals.

It takes the whole family for 5 plus generations doing all the things we have done individually and collectively. What a Wild Adventure with such rich experiences for us all. It has been my privilege to walk this path with Bill Long.

I dedicate this book to him and his family which is my family as he asked me to help him heal and so I have dedicated my last 10 years to accomplish this.

If my time on the Outlaw Trail is done in is with gratitude that I share what I have learned to do my part so that one Outlaw could heal and most into the light. If there is more to be accomplished, saddle up the ride into the roost is rough, wild, dangerous, exciting, amazing with twists and turns and surprises at every turn and behind every rock.

And so it is and so may it be done. With you Grandpa Bill we are honored to ride and with my fellow family members it's also an honor to ride with you and share this fascinating heritage which we have been gifted by birth with. I'm up to it, why become a boring family now? It's just not in our DNA.

CONFESSIONS OF A PSYCHIC WARRIOR SHAMAN

This journey was tough. Very tough. But, it was my chosen path. The Portal Access To Hyperspace through Remote Viewing had prepared me for the time when I met Bill Long's spirit. My passion for Remote Viewing was already developed and became invaluable as this journey proceeded.

Then it evolved into a passion for learning how to use intuition to truly empower one's life. Since I had some ability and was encouraged to use it by my mother who was a dreamer of prophetic dreams that came true, every time, I was dedicated to pushing the envelope and seeing how far I could take my gifts and make them useful.

I became a certified Hypno-therapist to maximize my understanding of how my mind works and the most advantages

ways of expanding my mind/body connections and how to bring to
fruition the most powerful, positive, progressive and profound
outcomes. Powerful mind, powerful intuition, powerful body,
powerful life. That's was my road map and heart's greatest desire,
to master this medium of intuition applied to real life.

Using hypnosis and then binaural beat recordings to expand
my neuro-net along with guided imagery, learning to activate my
heart intelligence and finding fascinating ways to apply these
abilities.

At one point, have had many, many successes most of which
were tremendously exciting to me, but not transferrable to the
outside world, yet. So, my next passion was using my intuitive
skills applying them is such a way as to come up with a adventure
of a life time where my work would be so "out of the box" AND at
the same time ONE SOLID GROUND...meaning verifiable to
someone besides myself.

Big stretch, but why take a small step when you can take a big
one? And a small step wouldn't produce the results powerfully
enough for people to "get it". And IT was so very awesome I
wanted to share all the remarkable experiences I have been
enjoying in intuitive/spiritual realms.

By 1999, April to be exact, my angel mother Faye who had
been telling about late night Art Bell and a new thing called
Remote Viewing that the secret government remote viewers had
been doing for 30 years started by some psychic named Ingo
Swann. She was passionate about remote viewing.

I was skeptical at first, but I loved my mother and so I
listened with her to Art Bell and his guests talking about Remote
Viewing including one who particularly impressed me as being a
reliable source of information name Lynn Buchanan. About that
time I wanted to learn Remote Viewing because I realized that if I
could get clear and accurate feedback about intuitive data that
would be phenomenal!

How much better decisions could I make in my life, how
much more fun and interesting...then I heard from my hypnosis
friend Teri about Dr. Simeon Hein coming to Salt Lake City, Utah
at Brighton to be exact to teach Remote Viewing. That was it. I
knew I had to be at that training so I took all the money I had and
signed up for his class in August of 1999.

Unbelievably heart expanding, mind expanding, experience expanding and that was just the beginning. As I Remote Viewed the first time, I put my pen to the paper and within a couple of minutes I "launched" into hyperspace intuitively. Such a tremendous experience which I only remembered the high points of because it was so soul expanding.

However, two of the most life changing understandings came back with me. One, was that I could access information this way any time I wanted to, I just had to go through the efforts to develop my skills and learn the medium. Two, no one could ever keep me out again. Not the clergy, not the gurus, not anyone...save myself being lazy and that wasn't going to happen any time soon.

The power inherent in the intuitive realms was now mine for the mastering and I have been thrilled with these skills and abilities and how much fun I can have with them since that moment. As I came back into the room, my consciousness became aware of being in Brighton, Utah, and a Remote Viewing training class. My instructor was sitting right in front of me.

I stared at him while my eyes readjusted to the room and started jumping up and down saying, "Simeon, did you know that anything you want to know is through this door? All you have to do is learn to go get it? Anything in space and time?"

Simeon just smiled that amazing smile he has when one of his students "gets it" and gave time to become adjusted to having been given the universe as my school room and creative intelligence that had nothing better to do than enlighten me as my teacher and guide. To me, this was heaven and I didn't even have to die to get there! How very cool is that?

Train I did, study, practice, practice, practice, got to seminars, meet the government remote viewers who were at the conferences. Clear Water Florida where I learned that I could tell what was taped under the seat of my chair. I could tell you how close the closest weapon was to me and if it was dangerous or not. Austin, Texas, where I really wanted to meet Ingo Swann, again he was the gifted psychic who developed the process of Remote Viewing for the secret government agency.

The lines to meet Ingo were much longer than I was willing to stand in so I decided to be content with observing from afar. An hour later, I got restless in one of the RV classes and wanted to find the most beautiful spot in the conference plaza. I went out into the atrium and went to the center to sit on the bench amid the beautiful greenery, flowers and butterflies.

No one was anywhere as I entered so I just relaxed and enjoyed the shimmering water babbling as it meandered through the plants. I climbed the last steps to be startled by the presence of someone...astoundingly, it was Ingo. The one person I wanted to talk to. He indicated I was welcome to sit with him and we talked for a few minutes. I asked al my questions. A most remarkable man with such a well trained mind. I was satisfied and then we moved on to the next part of the conference. These synchronicities became more and more common for me as I practiced Remote Viewing and my intuitive abilities expanded.

About this time was when I also spent a little time at a couple of Native American Ceremonies. I have Seneca Blood in me and once in a while it boils and I find myself wanting to participate in certain things. It was at one of these times, a certain peyote ceremony that everything changed. After a night of way out of the box experiences that strengthened me, healed my soul, expanded my understanding of everything, when the sun came up I was sitting on a hill outside of St. George, Utah enjoying the red rock cliffs when I shifted to experiencing sitting on a grid. A black onyx grid.

I asked what is this? Hoping someone would answer. "It's the Fabric of the Universe."

Wow, that was cool, someone cared enough about me to talk to me in this fascinating place. To make a long and remarkable story short, everything I wanted to experience was instantaneously appearing for me to enjoy and partake of. Sacred Geometric shapes wandered on by interacting with each other as them passed. I learned so much that morning in the sunshine on the red cliffs in St. George which totally redefined my life.

THE SHAMAN'S FIRE, CEREMONY BEGINS

By August of that year, I was in Duschesne, Utah, throwing my $350 nickel plated Smith and Wesson 9mm pistol in the river. It was the same river system that flows through to the Duschesne River. Now this is significant. This is where The Outlaw Trail begins to converge with my intuitive desires to bring something useful from hyperspace as the Remote Viewers call it into physical realms.

I had been at another Native American Peyote Ceremony but the shaman had pulled me out and had me join him in his tee pee. He hand me some coals from his fire and told me to take them down to the Duschesne River and was my hands in the coals then rinse them in the river. Strange request. I almost just left and went back to Salt Lake City, but I had to know if this was something real or just some mumbo jumbo. So, I took it to heart an did as Eric the Shaman requested. He also said, "You have unfinished business in the valley."

Me? What valley, uhhh...more details please. My mind was racing a million miles an hour. I chose to do as I was instructed, just in case it was real and would produce something real and interesting. I did my little ritual at the Duschesne River, oh, did I talk about the ostrich? Yes, there are two ostriches that live in Duschesne. On my was driving in on the dirt road past The Pinnacles, this ostrich appeared out of nowhere running straight at me at 30 mph. He got out of the way and when I stopped, he pecked at my shiny Black 2000 Ford Explorer. I'd rather he not do that, I liked my paint job just fine. But, he was much bigger than I, so I dedicated to just drive off slowly until he was out of range and went on the ceremony. I started to call him Eric after the Shaman.

That's how I met Eric, the Ostrich in Duschesne, Utah. I know, sounds unbelievable, but that's how my life flow began to take on an almost magical quality of synchronicities and really exciting, interesting and remarkably series of fun events, fascinating people and just plain fun times.

So after the Shaman's fire, I drove down to the Duschesne River as Eric the Shaman instructed, and who shows up? You guessed it, Eric the Ostrich who I had been addressing as the Shaman Eric. The only problem was I was not in my Explorer any more. I was standing knee deep in the Duschesne River having washed my hands of the coals of a Shaman's Fire.

Ok, negotiations with a large ostrich went something like this. I'm really glad you came to join my little ceremony here. Now, the

only problem is this river is getting cold and I want to get out. The next problem is you are much taller than I am and I don't have my Explorer to protect me. All I have is this little round drum. So, slowly I'll come out and you just watch from where you are.
My slow retreat from the icy waters of the river went well enough, except that left me 10 feet from Eric the Ostrich. Then he lifted his wing and plucked a feather which drifted to the ground. I had been receiving the most remarkable feathers across the United States from special places at special times and I considered this a special gift from the Universe. Except, it was 2 feet from Eric the really big Ostrich. Well, it was now or never...

Slowly I walked up to him, soon learned what made him nervous and what calmed him and looked the other way as I picked up the feather, gray, fluffy, so very soft. Forgetting to breath, I slowly back up and eventually made my way back to the safety of my Explorer under the intensely watchful eye of Eric the Shaman Ostrich.

Whew...safe. As I started my Explorer and pondered the direction I wanted to exit this great ceremony from, I turned my Explorer south along the river. I suddenly got the intense and indescribable feeling that I need to throw my gun in the river. Yep, you know the $350 Smith and Wesson, Nickle Plated perfect 9mm? I loved that gun.

I said, "No! Are you crazy? I love that gun. Absolutely not!"

Another half a mile and the intensity grew to throw my shiny revolver in the river. I almost did this time, thinking that it might be worth $350 to know for sure if this intuitive thing is real or not. For whatever reason I was being prompted (at least I thought I was being prompted by my intuition) ... Remote Viewing, Peyote Ceremonies meet The Sundance Kid and The Outlaw Trail. No, this is silly. I drove on.

After a few more bends in the road, the river still shimmering in the evening sun around each bend, the intensity grew even stronger. I decided that it was worth $350 to know it this was real and pulled out my clip, unloaded the chamber and the last thing I saw of my beautiful baby was its silvery body sinking into the river, lost from my grasp.

So, every day for the next year of my life, I woke up thinking how silly I was from throwing my perfectly good Smith and Wesson 9mm nickel plated pistol into the river. My husband, understandably, thought I'd lost my mind. I wasn't sure he wasn't correct some days.

I agonized over this for quite some time, them made peace with the fact that it was a decision I was willing to make and on my spiritual evolutionary path it was more important to know even if it cost me 350.00 and my shiny new Smith and Wesson 9mm nickel plated revolver, my baby.

One year to the month later, I got my answer. That was the best spent $350 of my life. Before I tell you why, let me go back two years from that day in Roosevelt, Utah when I was speaking to the grandson of William Henry Long, The Sundance Kid. His name was Roland Merkley. He was in an assisted living center and he, "Just wanted to know who his grandfather was."

His great grandfather was Christopher Merkley. Christopher Merkley was a polygamist out of Star Valley, Wyoming. In fact, in the year of the great snow, the killing snow as it was called in the Green River Valley of Wyoming, he was in the valley. The settlers were starving for want of supplies.

The store owner wouldn't give them credit or he would go broke by summer. Enter the dire picture coming in a heroes on a rescue mission were the unlikely pair of "supposedly cattle ranchers from Montana" Matt Warner and Tom McCarty. Of course they went by their alias identities because they were running from the law and ducked into Star Valley just as the snow buried them for the winter and no law man could get it.

Our heroic team of rescuers took the local Bishop into the local store and at gun point, had the Bishop take down the names and supplies these settlers needed to survive. Then they paid for half of the supplies and the people could pay for the other half when the snow melted. So, circumstances brought Christopher Merkley, great grandfather of Roland Merkley together with Matt Warner and Tom McCarty in their early years before the Wild Bunch was formed.

They were brothers-in-law and on the Outlaw Trail. They saved the lives of the settlers of Star Valley, Wyoming that winter. Strange the twists and turns of life. Yes, this is the same Matt Warner that rand with Butch Cassidy in the 1890's. Yes, this is the same Tom McCarty that taught Butch how to rob banks in Telluride, Colorado.

Roland was the grandson who would deliver milk to Grandpa and Grandma Long's house every morning. He was the one who found Grandpa Bill's body, dead on the wood pile that morning in November in 1936.

Two years before that day in Roosevelt when the revelation of revelations from Roland put everything that had happened to me in perspective. I'll get back with you on just what the revelation was in a minute.

August two years I was in Herriman, Utah when I first met the Ghost of the Sundance Kid and promised him I would help him heal and move into the light.

TIMING IS EVERYTHING

Sequence of Significant Events which lead me to writing this book about Ghosts, Outlaws, DNA and Polygamists.

1989-1999 A 12 Year-Long Dark Night of the Soul

According to Eckhart Tolle: THOSE WHO GO THROUGH A DARK NIGHT OF THE SOUL: "awaken into something deeper, which is no longer based on concepts in your mind. A deeper sense of purpose or connectedness with a greater life that is not dependent on explanations or anything conceptual any longer. It's a kind of re-birth. The dark night of the soul is a kind of death that you die. What dies is the egoic sense of self. Of course, death is always painful, but nothing real has actually died there – only an illusory identity. Now it is probably the case that some people who've gone through this transformation realized that they had to go through that, in order to bring about a spiritual awakening. Often it is part of the awakening process, the death of the old self and the birth of the true self."

I'm here to tell you, Eckhart Tolle had it pegged. This 12 year journey through shadow prepared me for what was to come. First the rebuilding of my mind, my heart, my consciousness. Then the enhanced intuitive trainings which launched my life experiences into a whole new category of Optimal Life Experiences.

1991 Hypno-therapy Training Virgil Hayes and The Hypnotism Center of Salt Lake City, Utah

August 1999 Remote Viewing Training from Mount Baldy Institute of Resonant Viewing

August 2002 Peyote Ceremony, Waking Up on the Fabric of the Universe

August 2003 Meeting the Ghost of Sundance

August 2004 Peyote Ceremony where I threw my gun in the Duschesne River System

August 2005 Roosevelt with Roland Merkley, grandson of Sundance and the Revelation about the gun that shot Bill Long being thrown in the Duschesne River, exactly one year after I had thrown my gun in the same river system

16 September 2006 Roland Merkley died in Roosevelt, Utah.

October 2006 Digging Up Bill Long's Bones, we did the first of three exhumations.

Now you are forming a road map through this amazing web of people, places and events, let's get back to the GREAT REVELATION which was so astonishing that it was beyond all boundaries and gave me my heart's greatest desires. To have something know in the intuitive realms manifest into physical realms and be so astonishing yet clearly profound that it would remove all doubt as to its presence in that form.

JEREMIAH MERKLEY THREW THE GUN THAT SHOT BILL LONG IN THE RIVER

We were speaking to Roland about his grandfather Bill Long's death. "And what did your dad, Jeremiah Merkley do with the gun the killed Bill Long?"

I heard Roland say, "My dad threw that gun in the river. We looked and looked for it and never found it."

That gun was thrown into the same river system, the one emptying into the Duschesne River. This was the same river system that I had thrown my gun into simply because I felt it was important for me to do so after the ceremony on the river washing the ashes off my hands from the Shaman Eric's fire with the Ostrich I call Eric the Ostrich Shaman. Same river system, just down the road a few miles.

Now tell me if it worth $350. Millions of times over, it was worth it. That I had the courage to take that risk to see if I was right about this still is deeply touching and amazing to me. And after a year the GREAT REVELATION OF ROLAND MERKLEY changed my life forever. Now I was completely dedicated to helping The Ghost of Sundance go wherever he thought he needed to go and do whatever he thought he needed to do.

What greater life mission could I ask for? It had been so much more interesting than anything I had been doing before and was a direct manifestation of the kind I was so wanting to experience and generate. How very awesome!

It was then that I found myself diving in with great earnestness searching for the true identity of William Henry Long, my ghost.

The Ghost of the Sundance Kid who wanted to heal, help his family heal and move into the light. He was done with feeling the heaviness and sadness of all he had experienced in his life. He moved on through into the light that night in Herriman and so shall we all join him if we so desire to progress.

CHAPTER 12

Historical Geocaching

Escape From Castle Gate

DO YOUR OWN DISCOVERY, TAKE YOUR OWN OUTLAW
TRAIL ADVENTURE

PLACES TO DISCOVER, INFORMATION AND DATA
SOURCES USED IN
GHOSTS, OUTLAWS AND POLYGAMISTS

HISTORICAL GEOCACHING

2016 The Escape From Castle Gate Calendar

It's a 12 hour geocache adventure complete with 12 sites that Butch Cassidy, Elza Lay and Bub Meeks followed through the San Rafael Swell. I spent 2 years with my 6th cousin ,Steve DeFriez who is a fellow Allred Family descendent, researching the San Rafael Swell and all of Emery County to find out where they really went.

Steve's grandfather, Paul Hansen, was 17 years old and herding 3,000 head of sheep in the San Rafael Swell, near Swayze's Leap when Butch Cassidy came through the day after the robbery and jumped the Leap. "Polly" as he was called, saw it all.

Historical Geocaching is a great way to see awesome country, learn about Utah history, share your Butch Cassidy and Sundance Kid stories and just have a great time.

Starting in Castle Gate, Utah and ending in Hanksville.

Ghosts, Outlaws, Polygamists and DNA
Outlaw Trail Adventures Genealogy Data Base
Introducing The First Etta that Butch Danced With
The Sundance Kid has many alias identities
DNA, The Science that proved who The Sundance Kid alias
William Henry Long who he isn't and who he is
Finding live descendents and revealing deep secrets of Wild West

Watch
https://www.facebook.com/OUTLAWTRAILADVENTURES
We will be revealing the coordinates for Outlaw Trail Adventure sites for the following:

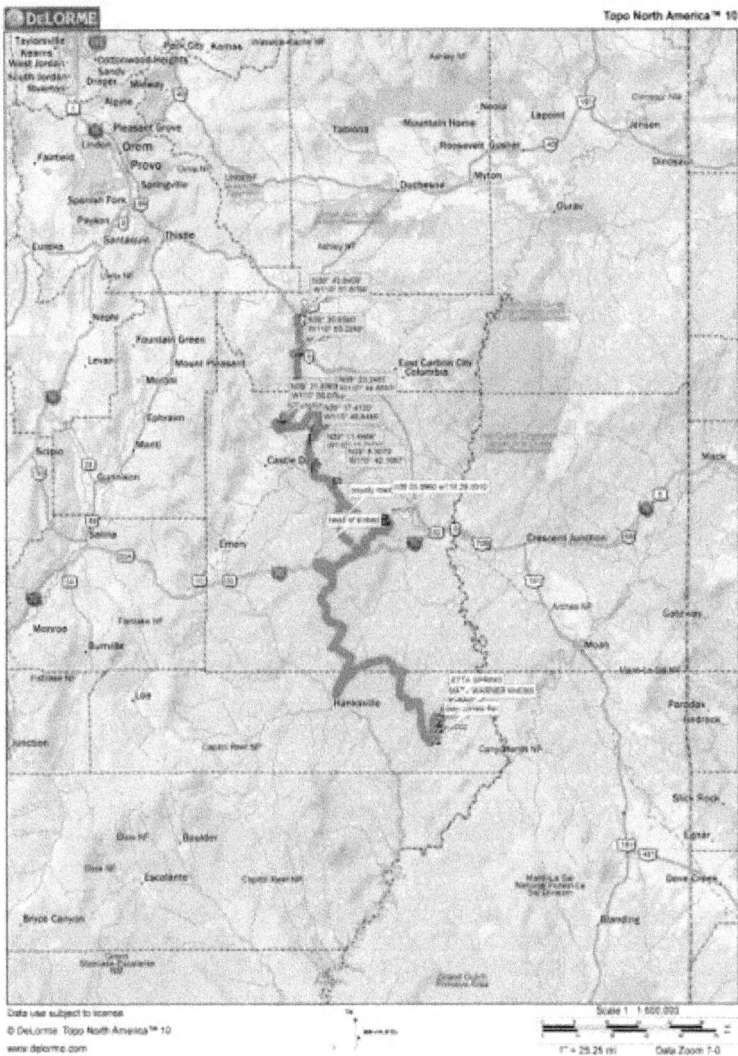

Historical Geocaching
Escape from Castle Gate (the Castel Gate Robbery April 29, 1897)

A 12 hours, 12 cache historical geocache run starting in Castle Gate, Utah and ending in Hanksville, Utah

Find the Escape From Castle Gate Historical Geocaching Calendar with exact coordinates, and the real history behind the Castle Gate Robbery 29 April 1897.

Emery County has given up its secrets for this Outlaw Trail Adventure. Get you copy now at www.outlawtrailadventures.com or see Steve De Friez in Castle Gate, Utah on 100 North 2nd house before you leave town on the road out to Orangeville…

Be careful though…he'll have you out chasing outlaws in the San Rafael Swell before you know what's happening…and loving every second of it!

More Historical Geocache Calendars on their way including:

Follow us on www.outlawtrailadventures.com or https://www.facebook.com/outlawtrailadventures/

Important Places on The Outlaw Trail:

We will have more Historical Geocache Calendars including:

BEAVER, UTAH, BUTCH CASSIDY'S BIRTH PLACE

JOSEPH, UTAH AND THE TRAIN TO COVE

FORT EPHRAIM AND THE BABY BUNCH, 1860

HANKSVILLE, UTAH AND CHARLIE GIBBONS STORE (shed is still standing)

GATEWAY TO ROBBERS ROOST

THE ROAD TO ROBBERS ROOST

SAN RAPHAEL SWELL, THE TRIAD: GREEN RIVER, MOAB, HANKSVILLE

ROBBERS ROOST THE IMPENETRABLE FORTRESS:

HAHNS FLAT RANGER STATION

TWIN CORRALS

TRAIL SPRING

SAND HILL ROBBERS ROOST

THE INNER CAMP

ETTA'S SPRING

MARY'S RESORT

THE KNOBS

THE WALL

S TURN

PRICE UTAH, MATT WARNER'S GHOST AT PRINT SHOP

SUNDANCE KID alias FRANK SMITH AND ETTA'S HOME

FISH SPRING 1900, FRANK AND JULIA ETTA SMITH

BABY WILLIAM, THEIR FIRST SON, DIES, BURIED IN
LYMAN CEMETERY

BY THE RAILROAD YARDS IN PRICE, UTAH

WAYNE COUNTY, LOA HOME OF THE SUNDANCE KID
ALIAS BILL LONG

SON-IN-LAW JERIMIAH JACKSON BLACKSMITH FOR THE
WILD BUNCH

LYMAN, UTAH SUNDANCE 2 LIVES NEXT DOOR TO
ETTA'S PARENTS
GROVER, FISH SPRINGS, ETTA AND SUNDANCE LIVE
1899
DANISH MEADOWS: BILL LONG'S CABIN
HOLE-IN-THE-WALL WYOMING, THE EARLY YEARS
BROWN'S HOLE, THE MIDDLE YEARS
BLOODY WATCH ON BOLDER MOUNTAIN, 2009

PEOPLE TO KNOW:

WILLIAM HENRY LONG ALIAS THE SUNDANCE KID BURIED IN DUSCHESNE, UTAH

Julia **Etta** Ames (Smith)

The Sundance Kid alias Frank Smith

The Sundance Kid alias William Henry Long

Luzernia Ann Allred (Morrell, Long)

Robert LeRoy Parker, Butch Cassidy

Ellis Eames, grandfather to Etta, his 3 wives

George Monteville Eames, father to Etta

Mary Callahan, step-mother to Etta

Rosina Ames, Sister to Etta

Mary Nadine Ames (Lazenby) half-sister to Etta

Walter Lazenby, brother-in-law to Etta, father of the wife of the step-son of Sundance

Ruby Lazenby (Morrell), wife of the step-son of The Sundance Kid alias William Henry Long

Hiatt Morrell, step-son to The Sundance Kid, William Henry Long

Ernest Morrell, step-son to The Sundance Kid, William Henry Long

Ephraim Hanks, settled Hanksville, rescued the Martin and Willie's Handcart Companies

Charley Gibbons, Banker for Butch Cassidy, store owner in Hanksville, Utah

Ellen Sophia Flanders, Etta's mother

Died in child birth when Etta was 3, 1879, Payson, Utah

Ellen Sophia Jacobs, Etta's grandmother, 1st husband Collins Eastman Flanders,

2nd husband Dimick Baker Huntington, main Indian Interpreter and right hand man to Brigham Young

His sister Prescendia Lathrop Huntington was sealed to the Prophet Joseph Smith by her brother Dimick Baker Huntington

His sister Zina Diantha Huntington was also sealed to the Prophet Joseph Smith in the Nauvoo Temple by Dimick Baker Huntington

Collin Eastman Flanders, maternal grandfather to Etta

Florence Viola Long, daughter The Sundance Kid alias William Henry Long

Evinda Long, daughter to The Sundance Kid alias William Henry Long

PLACES TO BE:

Joseph, Utah, 1880 and 1896
Fort Ephraim, Utah, Black Hawk Indian Wars, 1860-1865
Beaver, Utah 1850-52, 1866
Milford, Utah 1892-1894
Panguitch, Utah 1892
Circleville, Utah 1879
San Bernardino, California, 1850-1857
Hanksville, Utah, Charley Gibbons Store, 1890's
The Muddy Dubb, below Rico, Colorado May 1891
Fremont, Utah 26 Sep 1894, death of Silas Morrell, husband of Luzernia
Upper Pasture, finding Mary's Resort
Lower Pasture, finding the real inner camp
Hanksville, Utah, Charley Gibbons, Luzernia worked for him delivering supplies to The Roost
Jack's Point, Allred Trading Post Rabbit Valley
Silas Spring, the footprint of the ranch is still there
Danish Meadows, the footprint of Bill and Luzernia's Cabin are still there

This is where I'm going to leave you wandering in the San Raphael Swell looking for Ghosts, Outlaw, Polygamist and DNA until your heart's content. This is the first book. We have an Historical Geocaching Calendar: Escape From Castle Gate for 2016. The next calendar will take you deeper into Robber's Roost and The Impenetrable Fortress.

The next book will continue the adventures, there's much more you haven't even begun to see, YET...

May our paths cross on an Outlaw Trail Adventure where we can swap yarns and discuss the latest genealogy, science and DNA and talk about Ghosts. If you have the courage, may you find your own way to meet and experience Butch Cassidy, Sundance, Etta,

Tom and Bill McCarty, Matt Warner, Joshua Sweat, Bub Meeks their friends, and their families. These are:

The Ghost Riders of the Wild Bunch

The Key: Look for them among the living entities, those who are healing and moving into the light. If you engage with them, remember they are tough and they mean business. You are likely going to find yourself and your life spontaneously healing and self-correcting; this will get wild and dicey until you develop the spiritual muscles sufficient to ride with them into Robber's Roost. Take your medicine and ride for all you're worth.

It's a powerful and exciting journey when you ride with The Ghost Riders of the Wild Bunch.

WWW.OUTLAWTRAILADVENTURES.COM

https://www.facebook.com/OUTLAWTRAILADVENTURES

This has been a spiritual adventure on the Outlaw Trail. Thanks for joining my wild ride. See you in Robbers Roost!

ABOUT THE AUTHOR

Remote Viewing, Hypnosis and Holistic Practitioner have been my passions and profession for 30 years. In the middle of the intuitive skills I was fortunate to inherit a heritage that crossed the American Continent and settled the Wild and Wooly Territory of Deseret. For 15 years I have lived as series of Outlaw Trail Adventures to find the Outlaw World of Butch Cassidy, Etta Place and the Sundance Kid. I have published a book called, "Ghosts, Outlaws, Polygamists and DNA". My second great grandfather is The Sundance Kid.

Specialties: Remote Viewing, Hypnosis, Personal Transformations, passionate researcher on the Wild Bunch with Butch, Etta, Sundance and Tom, To facilitate training others is personal transformation and healing I created a series of workbooks used as a guide to Transforming our "Personal Monsters" to Profoundly Powerful Positive and Progressive techniques to help you achieve the transformation you seek.

I have been married to four great men who have supported me and strengthened me through an incredible life filled with profound and powerful relationships and experiences. I have had the honor to be mother to one son, five step-sons and one step-daughter, six grand children, 7 foster children, and have had the privilege of giving a loving place to live to many others from short periods of time.

I am very grateful for each of them and the profound impact for good they have had on my life and the great experience each of them are to me. Raising my children is the most rewarding and enjoyable part of my life.

Bambie's Free Flight Universe is about Stepping onto the Fabric of the Universe where you can Experience For Yourself Awareness, Awakening, Ascension and Wholeness, nothing lacking, enjoying Your Exquisite Nature.

PROFESSIONAL ACOMPLISHMENTS INCLUDE:

Professional Training and Certifications

Utah School of Hypnosis with Virgil Hayes, 1991
Certified Hypnotherapist

Mount Baldy Institute of Resonant Viewing 1999-2001
Level One, Level Two and Level Three Resonant Viewing
Certification

Member IRVA, International Remote Viewing Association since
2001

Advanced Remote Viewing Training with Dr. Angela Thompson
Smith and the Nevada Remote Viewing Group

Owner, Free Flight Universe Productions, January 1985 – Present
Salt Lake City, Owner, Professional Remote Viewer, Psychic,
Medium, Master Hypnotist.

Computer Professional, University of Utah, November 1991 –
April 2005 (13 years 6 months), Manager Scanning Center at the
Marriott Library, Developed the web evaluation program for the
University.

Manager Scanning Center, University of Utah, January 1991 –
April 2005

EDUCATION INCLUDES:

University of Utah, Studied Business and Psychology, January
1991 – April 2005

LDS Business College, Associates Degree specializing as a Legal
Secretary, June 1973– March 1975

Hillcrest High School, Business, DECCA Club, Choir, Drama, Fall
1973 – Spring 1973

Chapter 13

Spiritual Adventures Beyond The Outlaw Trail

THE VISIONS
THAT CHANGED MY LIFE FOREVER

My life is a series of synergistic and most remarkable web of connections showing up at the perfect time, whether I realize the perfection in the timing yet or not. It's always far better than I could ever have imagined and I have a great imagination. This is far better, real experiences that are build out of my heart's greatest desires. So, here are my visions. They were given in my most desperate hours and saved my life and my sanity more than once.

Here are my Spiritual Adventures Beyond the Outlaw Trail

My Free Flight Universe Spiritual Adventuress

I was blessed to be able to care for some great people in their final transition times in their lives. The great gifts I have received through it all are unbounded. The people that I have been able to help along the way have been another great gift in my life.

NDE's are a long time part of my life. My dear mother, Faye Rose, died and came back 5 times in her life. Each time she came back with phenomenal experiences to share with us and a new mission. She was told she didn't have to come back, but if she wanted to here was her mission. She was remarkable in every way, such an angel and a great blessing to me and my family.

The time before the last time she died, she came back to help my nephew Jason. Spirit told her she could die with honor now, but if she chose to go back, her oldest grandson, Jason, could use some help growing up. She chose to come back and they read native American stories together and bonded in a new way which was awesome for them both.

The last time she died and returned was in January 2004. She had a perforated colon which was about done after many, many years of challenging times. Her autoimmune system would attack her body with arthritis, lupus, and so on. MSM helped a lot and the Meda-tron Rattler which extended her life and significantly increased the quality of her life.

In fact what I learned trying so hard to help her, actually saved my own life this last year. I was able to help her significantly, but couldn't get it solved as much as I wanted to. I could now. The simple answers after years of trying many, many things and spending a lot of money on many things both traditional and non-traditional have given me a new lease on life.

If I start the day with 6 ounces of lemon juice, raw, organic as possible lemon juice and put 1 teaspoon baking soda in it, it bubbles up, then settles back down and I drink it on an empty stomach. This alone, cleared up most of my digestive and disintegrative issues. Then I soak in hot springs as much as possible which has saved my life many times for many years as a detox and healing measure.

Then if I watch my diet and avoid lactic acid foods, sugars and carbs of all types, grains of all kinds, and meats generally, I recover and feel great. After a month of this, I am able to eat some cheese, some bacon, some carbs, taking it easy and very moderate and I still am thriving. I had to trust my own intuitive instincts to get it all figured out. It's worth it. And I use MSM. The Walmart bottle of MSM is only 10 bucks but I have to use butter to be able to swallow it. I prefer Jarrow Brand MSM when I have enough money to afford it. I have taken as much as 40 a day when my antibody reactions are really dangerous and I have to stop them.

I do better when I have some Youngevity 90 for life every day, I'm old enough my body enjoys easily absorbed nutrition and can put some in my big ice mug which makes me thing I'm having a tasty drink on the road and gives me extra energy.

All of this has been an ongoing ceremony on mammoth proportions. But, considering no one else has overcome it as much as I have, I'm very grateful I have come here and learned this. If all you can afford is lemon juice and baking soda, you can get it under control.

If you want to know more, contact me at www.freeflightuniverse.com. This is only what works for me. You get to awaken and figure it out for yourself.

Momma's Vision of the Other Side

As I stepped off the elevator in Yavapai Hospital and found my mother's room, she was just waking up from a nap. She had just been through massive colon surgery to put her colon back together and save her life.

Her life-long challenges with auto-immune diseases had taken it's toll and using prednisone was the only thing that got her through. It was her choice of how to deal with it. It came at a price, one she knew may happen. Prednisone itself caused many challenges. It was just the lesser of two evils. It had helped cause the disintegration she now was facing.

Once I heard of her travail, I asked the Universe that if she made it back this time, she had the last 4 times, that she bring a vision to me that would help me understand her and people like her and how to help them.

She made it back and began to expound upon her most fascinating visions of the other side.

Faye Rose Hansen Nickle was a dreamer of remarkable dreams which came true. She always knew when someone in the family was going to have a baby, before they told anyone, sometimes before they were pregnant. One year, she had a dream in January of having lots of puppies and kittens. That year there were 6 grandbabies born in the family.

Much to rejoice about that year.

Anyway, in her vision of the other side she was shown a conveyor belt of skins…yes human skins…they were prepared for spirits which were going to be born into another life. Most of them were babies. She explained that most of us are still moving through long lifetimes and have to start over as babies to learn all we need to learn.

But some of the skins were adults. She explained that some of us have evolved enough to walk into another lifetime as an adult. We have learned enough in other lifetimes that we can begin our lessons in an adult body.

She watched as people's spirit would enter into the top of the head of the skin and then they would walk into their next life.

She then asked about people who didn't want to live any more. Spirit showed her those who were disintegrating into a dot…back into the energy field of the Universe. You don't have to grow and go on. You can just disintegrate into a dot. However, this is the most painful thing that you can do.

This one concept changed her and her understanding of life. When she came back, she significantly reengaged in life and worked to be more alive and vibrant until the day she died 6 months later. She was happier to be alive and have the opportunity to do something.

The next thing she wanted to see was God. She wanted to meet God. Her guide told her to "stretch your box". She started to push upwards and her "energy box" stretched up to where God's Castle was. On an evergreen mountain with white shimmering walls.

The guide said she couldn't go there now or she couldn't go back to her body. So, she was content and returned to her body and another shot a living life.

Poppa Meets a Being of Light

My father, Jack, was thrown from his motorcycle at 60 mph as he went over a metal grate and couldn't hold the turn. He had an extended NDE and was talking to a being of light about all of us. He hit the grate going too fast because he was too sad. His standing rule for riding motorcycles was when you were round up emotionally, you just don't ride. He broke his rule and that lead to his accident and his NDE. He received the guidance about each of his children, including me. Spirit said not to worry about me, I was just in the school of life and I would come out of it successfully.

He also told him he was taking too good care of my mother, his wife, Faye and that she was responsible for some of this and that he needed to help her become more self-responsible.

His vision and the changes he made after that made everyone's life better, however hard the changes may have seemed.

My Beloved Glen

My beloved husband, Glen Richardson, was very active during his death process and afterwards. We spoke extensively about communicating from beyond the veil here. The night he died from cancer, he left his body and I went with him, my spirit and his. I was laying next to him in the bed. As he reached through the veil, his father, Justin, was there. He had died years earlier.

Three days before Glen died, he asked me if I could get him out of here without all that mystical magical bullshit. I heard myself saying, "Yes." I had no clue how, but a deep part of me knew how and so we began.

I would hold his head as I guided him through a visualization that came to me as I was guiding Glen. It started by going towards a mountain in the distance and entering a pathway through a yellow portal. At the portal was a guardian that greeted us. There was a green portal where he left his world stuff, a blue portal where he finished his life business with everyone, then onward to a crystal portal on the top of the mountain and when he walked up the stairs he began to see a field full of butterflies and he followed the butterflies and heard a whole choir singing the Hallelujah Chorus. The last time he practiced this, he just didn't come back.

Many members of his beloved family were there to greet him. The last individual in a long line of greeters was a being of light at the Christ level of consciousness. He said to me, "Now you know how much everyone loves him, is it ok that he goes with us?" He was gently amusing and I could see through his eyes how I looked. I laughed with him and let Glen move on. I went back to my body. Just them, Glen's brother, John El, woke my body up and told me Glen had died.

Over the next year, Glen found delightful ways to contact me. The first thing I needed to learn was to look for his presence among the "living" energy fields. Just like he felt when he was physically with me. He got better and better at creating experiences which I would recognize as him and I got better and better at receiving his gifts and his continued love. My favorite, of so many,

My life has been filled with a richness of these experiences, some simply gifts and others experiences I sought after. All are appreciated and cherished. This spiritual path led me to a Native American Ceremony where I woke up on The Fabric of the Universe. Anything I asked to experience, was instantaneously manifesting. This experience has guided my life since that moment.

The Spiritual Gift of Outlaw Trail Adventures Was Given

When I desired to share my experiences, I asked for such a remarkable series of spiritual experiences that other people would enjoy learning about them and have fun implementing similar lessons in their own lives. This is what opened up from that intent and desire…Outlaw Trail Adventures.

For the last 10 years I have been on a most remarkable Outlaw Trail Adventure. I met the Ghost of the Sundance Kid and promised him I would help him heal. 10 years, thousands of miles and countless interviews later, it's time to tell all and finish the healing ceremony that began oh so long ago in that old round rock house in Herriman when a young man wanted to "just talk to a ghost." Delightful, delicious, exceptional and really fun, my life has unfolded like never before.

The spiritual path I desired was given and has it ever been a wild, wild, wild ride. I've loved every second of it. So, here you are, raw and wriggling. Now, it's your turn. Get on your horse and take The Outlaw Trail Adventure of your own, going wherever your heart and soul leads you, focused on your highest outcomes and grandest of adventures.

This is your adventure of a lifetime…see you on the trail. Experience your own PATH, Portal Access To Hyperspace holding your powerful, progressive, profound focus on exactly what you want to experience, hold it, hold it, hold it until your experience it or something better.

I feel fantastically alive, vibrant, healthy, happy and whole by choice, focus and receiving my gifts. Join me on the Fabric of the Universe, Let's Dance.

One day I just wanted to see God. So I prepared myself by contemplation, meditation with binaural beat recordings and setting my heart's desire then focused on:

THE THRONE OF GOD

I know it seems strange that I would start with a vision about The Book of Mormon, since it isn't obvious how this vision fits perfectly into my philosophy and life. Well, actually, my journey through religion and the Mormon Church serves me very powerfully. It is my Sacred Path. It's not mine yet to have the wisdom of why this was my highest path, why it lead to where it did and how it all intermingles and unfolds in great stories of intrigue, mystery, action and adventure. And I don't need to figure it out any more, it just is and it works perfectly.

I'll do my best to explain it. Being overzealous in most things I endeavor to master, especially anything having to do with spirituality and intuition. My intense focus was applied to studies of Joseph Smith, especially his own version of his visions. No more had I begun to read them when I was carried away in spirit to being interactive with his experiences, especially the pre-existence and being intelligences all considering our soon to come Earth experiences.

We were all equal in the Council in Heaven in power and so on save those who had more wisdom to progress and because they had this it became their work and their glory to help those of us who weren't as intelligent as they. However, everyone in that matrix of creation was equal in value, those who knew more sought to enlighten the rest.

Many were the experiences that came to me in answer to my earnest desires and prayers. Most often, especially in the beginning, much studying of sacred texts, fasting and prayer were needed to reach the state of consciousness that connected me to that living, loving, powerful source at the time I experienced according to my belief system as God.

Now, one day I really, really, really wanted to meet God, Father, Elohim. I know that seems presumptuous, however, it was in my heart and mind to do so. I hadn't been denied my honorable heart's desires to experience so far, I should at least try. The worst that could happen is I would be burned to a crisp or banned to outer darkness forever, neither of which made sense so I risked it.

After much fasting, sacred study, prayers and more prayers I was deep in meditation and prayer when my vision opened up and I was in an energy field of golden energy. I tried to make out shapes, but it occurred to my mind the understanding that here shapes were secondary. They could be taken but would only be used when there was a worthy purpose. The natural state here was energy plasma with consciousness about it. There was much collective thoughts here, yet individuals still retained their own thought space and individual identity in an advanced form.

I was looking for the Throne of God when I beheld a huge energy charge rise before me and for a large, golden throne for Father. I realized that it formed in answer to my desires to experience. How amazing! An interactive Celestial Kingdom, who would have thought. The presence of Father was permeating and comforting as he prepared my consciousness to understand and experience what I had desired to understand.

I felt full, happy, content, acknowledged, appreciated, enjoyed, nourished...all good things. I felt at one with Father and at peace with the Matrix of Creation which he used to generate the realities we know as life. How absolutely remarkable is that?

Then I found myself having returned from Eternal Glory to process and proceed in my life having obtained clear and accurate feedback about God Himself. I understood and was thrilled by the fact that God was my creator, my Father, my guidance. It is this that I cherish, his love and guidance. Yet there was no division between the Divine Masculine and Divine Feminine energies. It was the perfect balance and flow of creation, form which is masculine and flow which is feminine. No one controls this, it just is.

We can access what is and experience our own divine creative natures, our exquisite natures, but we cannot control what is, it just is. Again, we can access, experience, engage and expand into our own Wholeness which is inclusive of all that is. The rest is just thoughts about what is, beliefs about what is, philosophies about what is. What is, is. Once we have the courage to experience what is in it's purest forms and are really brave enough to do the soul expansion process until we are able to experience our Wholeness, this is our nature. We are the only ones who can keep us from being all that we are.

It was then that I left Heaven and knew there would a price to pay for believing. Though it would be worth it, oh, so worth it. The price was pure ceremony. Free Flight Ceremony. Powerful, pure, directly connected to source. Exquisite. It is our Exquisite Nature to live in a fullness of Free Flight, directly flowing from source, openly creating form...

This is where the rubber hits the road spiritually, emotionally, physically. This is it. Once you cease to fight your exquisite nature and embrace your exquisite nature, it begins. You can start, stop, start, stop, forever. It's all up to you. ENGAGE, EXPERIENCE, EVOLVE, ENJOY. That's it. This is one of my first visions.

The Fabric of the Universe

For 6 weeks before the peyote ceremony I dreamed a stream of dreams preparing me for the experience. I had never used any kind of substance because I wanted to experience spirit directly without any question as to what the source might be.

But I have Seneca Indian blood in my veins and it began to call out to me to find a peyote ceremony. I didn't believe in using peyote at the time, but my ancestors' energy was powerful and I came to understand it was important for my development.

I said, "You'll have to bring it to me, I have not clue and no connections and beside, I live in Utah."

Well, 3 days later my good friends asked me if I was interested in a peyote ceremony with Don Andreas, a Sonoma Shaman. Of course I said yes and was astounded, yet again.

To make a long stream of dreams and profound experiences short, by the time the sun came up and I felt the cold water in my face I had taken enough peyote to launch met into a profound vision state.

The room disappeared and I was on the Fabric of the Universe. I sat there feeling this live intelligence waving in a grid which looked like black onyx to me.

Nothing happened. Notta… until I questioned, "What is this?"

THE FABRIC OF THE UNIVERSE

I asked, "Does it do anything?"

WATCH

As I watched a large sphere rolled across the grid.

Awesome, I though.

"Does it do anything else?" I asked.

WATCH

All sorts of sacred geometrical shapes, the plutonic solids, moved across the fabric, interacting with each other and the fabric.

WOW! I though. Then I got bored...

"Okay, does it do anything else, what about male and female energy?"

Woosh...a male and an female all in this black onyx grid energy appeared interacting. When one moved, the other responded.
Very Awesome. But soon even that became boring to watch.

So I said, "If I have to look at this forever, I'll go crazy. Can I see something more interesting?"

Woosh... I found myself inside a huge golden mean spiral shaped shell lined with self-illuminated rubies and diamonds...shimmering...energizing...so very beautiful. I was content for a while.

Then even that beauty became boring. Is there anything more dynamic...you know...alive? Dynamic?

Woosh a man door appeared in the side of the shell. I knew if I opened the door, I never would be the same and couldn't go back. A split second later I had the door opened and was going out into....Space Odyssey 2001...the whole monolith, moneys, astronauts ...life as we knew it and I was thrilled!

I was thirsty for this life experience.

A year later I woke up form a dream and knew that anything I wanted to experience I got to experience instantly and that's how this really really works. Just fortunately we have a few built in safeguards so we don't hurt ourselves while we learn to master or creative power over reality.

My Beloved Father

There are times in every life and every family where challenges seem to outweigh our abilities to deal well with them.

Again, I'm revealing my innermost treasures of life experience through this whole book.. Sacred things. Profound changes in my life and the lives of others came out of these experiences. So what does sacredness and challenges have to do with each other?

Sacred Ceremony is a process that I have channeled over time, practiced, channeled more. Learned more from others, practiced more, and over time I evolved to unbelievably wild and interesting series of people, places, ideas and events that paraded before me and became my life.

At this time I am revealing the vision I call, "My Beloved Father."

It was only one block, howbeit a country block here in Midvale, Utah. Brigham Young, the first government that was established in the Territory of Deseret was established by Brigham Young. He was a great colonizer and meticulously made sure the streets were laid out so a team of oxen pulling a wagon could turn around in the street. So, the streets of Salt Lake City, Utah are generally a nice width. We lived on 1000 East about 7600 South.

Just down the road to the North, my Second Great Grandfather, Silas Richards, settle in the 1850's in the Cottonwoods. He built a fort along with the other families in his stewardship and they settled the Territory.

To the south of our home, my paternal grandparents, Clayton Jackson Nickle and Luzernia Jackson Nickle, had built a home. Grandpa Clayte built the home during the depression when building material was scarce. He found some railroad ties and built the entire home from railroad ties. It's a touch house. It was a one mile walk from our home on 1000 East south to where my grandmother, Luzernia Jackson (Nickle, Baker) lived. I had been fasting and praying which always brought clarity and strength of understanding to my mind and my soul.

Father had been acting in ways which didn't fit in my belief system about what he ought to be doing, especially in regards to religion.

What I believed he should be doing seemed so set in stone in my mind that I had been studying the scriptures, fasting and praying for two weeks to find a resolution that would be inspired by God because I loved my father dearly and what I believed I needed to do according to the scriptures and the general guidance of the clergy would have devastating impact on my father and our relationship would be trashed, probably for the rest of our lives.

This weighed upon my consciousness so heavily that I finally decided to do "what was right" according to my guidance from the scriptures and confront my father. My mother at the time was bedridden and the heavy burdens upon the family were a drain to all of us. We were making it through and figuring it out, learning and growing, but it was very difficult some days.

Under these circumstances, I was pleading with God to help me. I explained in my prayers that I believed I needed to confront my father but that would destroy our life together for he would feel attacked, rightfully so, and the turmoil that raged within me was overwhelming.

So, on a sunny Sunday afternoon, after church, I walked down the my grandmother's house because I knew my father was visiting her on his new Gold Wing motorcycle. It was absolutely gorgeous metal flake maroon with emblems painted on it and the words "Freedom Three" on the back of the trunk.

Poppa loved to ride. He personally wore out 5 Honda Gold Wings in his lifetime. So, it was with a heavy heart and a pleading soul I continued to seek guidance as I made my sad journey to confront my father. If I didn't my scriptures said my soul would be unworthy and I would not make to my eternal reward because I didn't confront what was presented to me.

Alas, as I walked with determined steps towards his motorcycle glimmering in the morning sun I continued to pray. "If this is the right thing, then help me be sure and do this well. If it is the wrong thing to do, then stop me. Do not let me reach that motorcycle. I'm following all the guidance you have provided for me and this is the answer. So, please help me."

By this time, I was half way there passing Tueller's house with the dog barking. All of a sudden Christ appeared right in front of me, halting my progress. I was swept away in vision state with Christ standing between me and my father's "Freedom Three" Gold Wing. I asked him what to do and spoke of my challenge.

As he looked into my soul through my eyes, I felt absolute clarity fill my being. Love beyond measure filled my heart. In this state of awakening to the pure love of Christ, he was holding my father as he was when he was an infant. Brand new, undefiled. He let me hold him and my heart and soul melted. There was no judgment on the part of Christ, only unconditional love. I knew my answer and with tears streaming down my face, I could see my father as an adult, coming out of grandma's house.

He saw me and came up to me, giving me a big hug, telling me he loves me. He let me know that whatever happens in the next while, we'll pull through it just fine. The most important part was to remember we love each other and are family who care about each other.

My soul melted into unconditional love and rapport. I had no more inclination to judge him or anyone ever again. If Christ could see his true nature then that is how I would hold him. Such a huge relief upon my heart and mind. My life and my relationship with my father were much improved and from that moment to this, I put down a burden of belief which were too heavy and built in shadow anyway.

There are times in every life and every family where challenges seem to outweigh our abilities to deal well with them. Again, I'm revealing my innermost treasures of life experience through this whole book.. Sacred things. Profound changes in my life and the lives of others came out of these experiences. So what does sacredness and challenges have to do with each other?

Sacred Ceremony is a process that I have channeled over time, practiced, channeled more. Learned more from others, practiced more, and over time I evolved to unbelievably wild and interesting series of people, places, ideas and events that paraded before me and became my life.

At this time I am revealing the vision I call, "My Beloved Father."

It was only one block, howbeit a country block here in Midvale, Utah. Brigham Young, the first government that was established in the Territory of Deseret was established by Brigham Young. He was a great colonizer and meticulously made sure the streets were laid out so a team of oxen pulling a wagon could turn around in the street. So, the streets of Salt Lake City, Utah are generally a nice width. We lived on 1000 East about 7600 South.

Just down the road to the North, my second great grandfather, Silas Richards, settle in the 1850's in the Cottonwoods. He built a fort along with the other families in his stewardship and they settled the Territory.

To the South of our home, my paternal grandparents had built a home. Grandpa Clayte built the home during the depression when building material was scarce. He found some railroad ties and built the entire home from railroad ties. It's a touch house. It was a one mile walk from our home on 1000 East south to where my grandmother, Luzernia Jackson (Nickle, Baker) lived. I had been fasting and praying which always brought clarity and strength of understanding to my mind and my soul.

Father had been acting in ways which didn't fit in my belief system about what he ought to be doing, especially in regards to religion. What I believed he should be doing seemed so set in stone in my mind that I had been studying the scriptures, fasting and praying for two weeks to find a resolution that would be inspired by God because I loved my father dearly and what I believed I needed to do according to the scriptures and the general guidance of the clergy would have devastating impact on my father and our relationship would be trashed, probably for the rest of our lives.

This weighed upon my consciousness so heavily that I finally decided to do "what was right" according to my scriptures and their guidance and confront my father. My mother at the time was bedridden and the heavy burdens upon the family were a drain to all of us. We were making it through and figuring it out, learning and growing, but it was very difficult some days.

Under these circumstances, I was pleading with God to help me. I explained in my prayers that I believed I needed to confront my father but that would destroy our life together for he would feel attacked, rightfully so, and the turmoil that raged within me was overwhelming.

So, on a sunny Sunday afternoon, after church, I walked down the my grandmother's house because I knew my father was visiting her on his new Gold Wing motorcycle. It was absolutely gorgeous metal flake maroon with emblems painted on it and the words "Freedom Three" on the back of the trunk.

Poppa loved to ride. He personally wore out 5 Honda Gold Wings in his lifetime. So, it was with a heavy heart and a pleading soul I continued to seek guidance as I made my sad journey to confront my father. If I didn't my scriptures said my soul would be unworthy and I would not make to my eternal reward because I didn't confront what was presented to me.

Alas, as I walked with determined steps towards his motorcycle glimmering in the morning sun I continued to pray. "If this is the right thing, then help me be sure and do this well. If it is the wrong thing to do, then stop me. Do not let me reach that motorcycle. I'm following all the guidance you have provided for me and this is the answer. So, please help me."

By this time, I was half way there passing Tueller's house with the dog barking. All of a sudden Christ appeared right in front of me, halting my progress. I was swept away in vision state with Christ standing between me and my father's "Freedom Three" Gold Wing. I asked him what to do and spoke of my challenge.

As he looked into my soul through my eyes, I felt absolute clarity fill my being. Love beyond measure filled my heart. In this state of awakening to the pure love of Christ, he was holding my father as he was when he was an infant. Brand new, undefiled. He let me hold him and my heart and soul melted. There was no judgment on the part of Christ, only unconditional love. I knew my answer and with tears streaming down my face, I could see my father as an adult, coming out of grandma's house.

He saw me and came up to me, giving me a big hug, telling me he loves me. He let me know that whatever happens in the next while, we'll pull through it just fine. The most important part was to remember we love each other and are family who care about each other.

My soul melted into unconditional love and rapport. I had no more inclination to judge him or anyone ever again. If Christ could see his true nature then that is how I would hold him. Such a huge relief upon my heart and mind. My life and my relationship with my father were much improved and from that moment to this, I put down a burden of belief which were too heavy and built in shadow anyway.

Through the remainder of our lives which spanned another 50 years, this experience with Christ was so profound, it carried me through challenges that tore at the very fabric of my consciousness. This powerful experience redefined all my relationships and enriched my life experience many fold. This unconditional experience of my father as an innocent baby guided me through every dark shadow that crossed our paths back to light and knowledge of all things exquisite.

I am prompted now to leave this book in its current form and move on to the second book specifically focused on visions, near death experiences and spiritual evolution. My third book will be a resurrection and expansion of my original works called, "Shadow Rising, The Antidote." I lovingly call them my "Monster Books." Through this third book of my spiritual trilogy Ghosts, Outlaws, Polygamists and DNA Books One, Two and Three, one can expand beyond the limits of the shadow matrix and the death programming. Waking up on the Fabric of the Universe, experiencing you Exquisite Nature and Embracing your creative empowerment in the Universe are all simply accomplished in a natural process I call Sacred Ceremony.

It seems the Universe thinks we're pretty awesome and gives us many tools with which to enjoy and decipher the Universe around us. It trusts us to figure this all out and embrace our greatest human traits. In wisdom and power we honor you all…

You have an open invitation to come right on in, sit down a spell, take your shoes off, enjoy some food and tell us your best stories. This is the times of our lives. I'm feeling fantastically alive, vibrant, Healthy, happy, whole. Powerful, positive, progressive, profitable and profound are my action guiding virtues and I empower myself with them with every breath.

If you have had a great time on the Outlaw Trail, stay with me for guidance on acquiring and becoming empowered with your own personal vision quest and subsequent mission in the Universe.

Stuck in a Dark Night of the Soul? Sacred Ceremony has the power to sustain you and strengthen you so you have the power to grock, grapple and grow overcoming all influences of the Shadow Matrix and becoming empowered on all levels. My cute little monster books will guide you every step of the way. My 6 year old nephew, Spencer, leads the way in Shadow Rising, The Antidote.

Trust yourself, you know the way and if you don't yet, you will soon. This I knew about you. If you are attracted to this reading, there is a purpose and you will be empowered, enlightened and enlivened with exactly what you need in this moment. Whatever baby step you need to allow the creative

intelligence to flow freely through every cell in your body once more, and so it is. Or not. This is my ghost story and I've told it like it is here on the Fabric of the Universe with Bambie Z. Be creative, be brave, be strong. Be wise, be loving, be awake, aware and actively creating your
Life as you see fit…step into your wholeness, it's within your power.

See you out there on the playa of life…the very fabric of the universe.

Let's Dance…

Our community is committed to a radically participatory ethic. We Believe that transformative change, whether in the individual or in society can occur only through that medium of deeply personal participation. We achieve being through doing. Everyone is invited to work. Everyone is invited to play. We make the world real through actions that open the heart.

So what does all this have to do with Ghosts, Outlaws, Polygamy and DNA? What has this got to do with visions, spirituality and personal transformation and evolution?

What you believe you can achieve and experience. My journeys through life that brought me the opportunity to ride The Outlaw Trail Adventures which have been amazingly thrilling as I met and overcame challenge after challenge with new doors of experience unfolding before me.

It's an honor to know you. Take the experience and ride on Outlaw Trail Adventures for yourself, you'll never be the same and you'll understand more about life than you ever thought possible. See you on the Trail!

My original journey into the realms of spirituality, visions, ghosts and remote viewing was an experiment of life experience. I chose to take the journey and see just what I could experience for myself.

Really, this all started as an experiment. After a while, the experiences became so remarkable and undeniable and reproducible that shifted my focus from an experiment on energy realms and "out of the box" first hand experiences to a focused "intent to experience" from this point of view...living my life in the flow so exquisite and sweet, so powerful and profound. And so it is now my life in an ongoing Outlaw Trail Adventure...for there is a little Outlaw in All of Us.

My Own Wholeness and Christ

And my favorite vision that saved my consciousness and changed my life path forever. This experience put me squarely outside the parameters I was supposed to be experiencing according to my religion, but I had outgrown the need for external validation by the time I returned from my vision. And what I came back with was so much more than I have ever conceived of and it transformed me to a most joyful state of being that I have never disintegrated from. This became my standard and it empowers me still.

It began with a two week depression and a desire to no longer exist. Now this was not normal for me, I had never experienced it before, however, I was experiencing it now. I had always been open to hanging in there and making good whatever I had been given. This time, I didn't want to any more.

At the bottom of that barrel I was in a tunnel, a dark tunnel and all I could see was a round while spot way up and I was trying to make it go out.

I had the presence of mind for some reason to say, If anyone cares enough to help me, now would be good.

Woosh…I was carried away to the Mormon Tabernacle on Temple Square downtown, Salt Lake City. A place I had been many times. I had even sang in the Soprano choir seats by the great tabernacle pipe organ in high school choir.

Now I found myself alone in the front row of a quite tabernacle. I was waiting for someone.

As I sat there I noticed some black stone spickies sitting around on the floor. I thought, "This will never do in a sacred place like this." And I picked them up. I had a whole handful of them and was looking for a garbage can to throw them into.

None to be found. I looked for a janitor to give them no. None to be found. I sat back down and reached down to set them on the floor in a neat pile to be picked up when the cleaners came.

Just as I reached to set them down, they began to move in my hands. I pulled them back up and began to wonder and watch them move in my hands.

As I watched, soon they began to break open and inside each on was a self-illuminated diamond, shimmering brilliantly. I realized these were very valuable. In fact, they were so valuable they must belong to someone very important, even Christ.

As this became evident to me, I wondered how I could get them to Christ. At that moment, he appeared in front of me.

I kneeled down on my right knee and lifted my hand above my head as I bowed my head and gave them to Christ. To my astonishment, he cradled my hands in his and lifted me up to look at him.

I could feel the love and warmth in his hands loving me beyond anything I had ever felt before. He then took the shimmering crown the diamonds had formed above my hands and placed upon my head and he said, "These are yours."

They circled above my head, then spread shimmering all over my plain house dress became and beautiful gown shimmering with self-illuminated diamonds and I experienced my complete wholeness. I was equal to Christ.

He told me, "You will not be counted less for anything you have experienced in your life."

And I knew that what he said was absolutely true. This wholeness has stayed with since then. I am free and joyful to experience life in it's fullness, whatever that means to me and I keep expanding my ability to enjoy life in it's ever amazing and diverse experiences.

And so it is…

www.ingramcontent.com/pod-product-compliance
Lightning Source LLC
Chambersburg PA
CBHW031253090426
42742CB00007B/428